Grandkids
as
Gurus

LESSONS FOR GROWNUPS

SUSAN LEBEL YOUNG

Library of Congress Catalog Card No.: 2020944608

Young, Susan Lebel
Grandkids as Gurus: Lessons for Grownups
Susan Lebel Young

1. Family & Relationships / General
I. Title

p.188
Softcover: 978-1-944386-52-8
Kindle: 978-1-944386-53-5

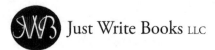 Just Write Books LLC

www.jstwrite.com
Topsham, ME 04086
Printed in the United States of America

Dedication

*To children everywhere
please keep shining,
keep teaching your lessons
in wisdom and compassion.
We need you.
The world needs you.*

What people are saying about Grandkids as Gurus

"An engaging, refreshing reminder of why we're all here. With humility, sensitivity, and 'deep bweffs,' Susan Lebel Young flips the script about elders as teachers. With profound presence, she highlights opportunities for learning and growing through the gifts inherent in these wise souls called grandchildren. From school to storytime; from fort-building to bedtime, we're treated to endless opportunities for reawakening our own childhood wonder, curiosity and joy. The writing is deeply relatable. The anecdotes are laugh-out-loud adorable. And the flashbacks to Young's own childhood and motherhood add even more depth to an already powerful read. Even if you're not a grandparent, this book will help lead you back home to yourself."

—Elisa Boxer, journalist & author of *The Voice that Won the Vote*

"Children laugh on average 400 times a day,; adults 40. Becoming an adult does not mean giving up wonder, joy and curiosity. In this book of listening and observation, Susan Young relates glimmers of the original self of childhood which we all carry within us hidden beneath the self we built to cope with the adult world. Dive in and recall what will enrich your life."

—George Dreher, MD

"We all love our grandchildren but Susan Young has taken the opportunity to let love listen to them, to let herself be moved and transformed by them. Susan uses her deep spiritual practice as a lens to show us *Grandkids as Gurus*. In chapters organized by themes like, 'Beginner's Mind,' 'Joy,' and 'Stop Adulting,' she gives us vignettes of her experiences of being with her grandchildren and her ways of loving them that all grownups—grandparents or not—will understand."

—Patricia Dodd Hagge, Nana to four grandsons, meditation
teacher, former Telling Room teacher and volunteer

"It takes a wise and attentive grandparent to move beyond delight in her grandchildren's sayings to seeing their inherent wisdom, wisdom even for guiding adults. Sue Lebel Young is that singular grandparent, and the result of her careful listening and disarming insights is *Grandkids as Gurus*. It should prove thought-provoking for her readers of all ages."

—Peter Monro, former journalist and blogger
at DesignForWalking.com

"Like most adults, Susan Lebel Young thought she knew how to be a grandparent. It turns out she really didn't. But she does now—thanks to her grandchildren/gurus. They have taught her 'Joy,' 'Kindness,' 'Patience,' 'Presence,' and other lessons that Young took to heart and captures in short, simple, but insightful anecdotes in *Grandkids as Gurus*.

The book speaks to adults of all age—whether or not they are grandparents. With her ability to find deeper meaning in the tender, touching, loving, and humorous interactions with her grandchildren, Young has crafted a handbook for grownups. As she says in the Preface, 'Children know. They sense. They feel.' May we bow to the true teachers. May this book help us listen to the kids and invite the adults to be learners. Life might be better. Way better."

—Mo Mehlsak, veteran Maine newspaper reporter & editor and grandfather of Noa, who teaches him daily

"In *Grandkids as Gurus*, Susan Lebel Young, offers the world a gift—a reminder of the wisdom and power of children—and a hearty nudge for all of us grown-ups to slow down and listen. With incredible compassion, and keen observation, Sue invites us to share everyday and profound interactions with her grandkids. In her unique voice, like an old friend, Sue encourages us to look to our youngest gurus for a roadmap for living."

—Stephanie McSherry, founder, Merry Barn Writers' Retreat

"Susan Lebel Young's *Grandkids as Gurus: Lessons for Grownups* is a wonder of a book both charming and utterly profound as one grandmother chronicles the practice of incidental devotion, revering the wisdom she gleans from her four grandchildren as they grow. From the unique voice of the narrator who we come to count on as Susu, readers will be entertained by the antics of 'Bob, Fred, Laudie, and Cookie' as the pages fly by. But these vignettes do more than simply enchant. They deliver an impact that makes me want to run out and notice all the magical moments that surround us, the ones we discover when we slow down enough to pay attention, the ones that invite us to be more attentive, more loving, more kind. Not since Ross Gay's *The Book of Delight* have I read a missive that offers this much everyday hope in an increasingly bittersweet world."

—Jodi Paloni, author of *They Could Live With Themselves,* writer, editor, creativity coach

"Susan Lebel Young's *Grandkids as Gurus* is a fun, and sometimes poignant, celebration of the innate and uncomplicated wisdom of children, and the dharma they offer us in each encounter. By generously sharing experiences with her own grandkids/gurus, we witness how toddlers and little kids can be teachers simply by being in touch with themselves, always in the present and without judgment. My big take away from this charming book is about letting go: while we perseverate, kids have moved on to whatever is next and interesting in their lives—often with no connection to what came before. Spontaneity is a way of being, not something to strive or apologize for."

—Maggie Butler, author of *Compassionate Journey: Honoring Our Mothers' Stories* and others

Contents

Gratitudes

Piglet noticed that even though he had a Very Small Heart,
it could hold a rather large amount of Gratitude.
—A.A. Milne, Winnie-the-Pooh

To my family for listening to me talk about this book for years and supporting me through it. I love you, deeply. Thank you.

To my publisher Nancy E. Randolph at Just Write Books, for wisdom, humor, expertise, time, energy and the love of this project. Thank you.

To my writing teachers over the years: Joan Hunter, Dulcie Witman, Jodi Paloni, David Kuchta, Maggie Butler. For your gateless creativity and wide-open minds and hearts. Thank you.

To my countless writing partners in group after group. For listening, for encouraging, for your writing which lifted mine, thank you.

To my four grandchildren. One of the greatest joys in crafting this book was hanging out with you, your friends, family, neighbors and babysitters. Thank you for showing me what real means, for showing me how to tell the truth. Thank you for your cuddles and hugs through "Read us more, Susu, one more story." Brilliant editors, you critiqued and tweaked the essays. For fun, we changed your names for this book. For big fun, you chose them. We laughed at your genius and creativity. We clapped at your scrappy courage. I am a better me because of you. Bolder. Wiser. Nicer. Sillier. I smile more. You taught me to slow down and love life now as it shows up in the magic of snowflakes, in the care of bugs, in the awe of this mud puddle, and in the jumps and bumps in pillow forts.

My final and most important thank you with air-finger quotation marks goes to "Bob, Fred, Laudie and Cookie."

Preface

It is tiresome for children to be always and forever explaining things to them [adults].
—*Antoine de Saint-Exupery,* The Little Prince

Cocooned in puffy comforters with my grandchildren one night, I read to them one of this book's essays. It highlighted a years-ago raucous pre-bedtime evening. All four of them in the bathtub. Blowing bubbles. Squirting rubber fishies. We giggled a little, howled a lot. I read a line about my choice in that bathtub moment to focus on their light rather than the "darkness in the world they will inherit."

Laudie, age seven in second grade, punched up her right hand and groaned, "Oh. Ugh. Susu. Stop. Stop right there. You gotta get rid of that."

"Get rid of what?" I asked.

"The darkness," she said.

"The darkness?" I repeated.

She pretended to cast a fishing line. "You hooked us in the beginning, telling the story of how we bobbed up and down, how we played 'sink the ship.' Then you reeled us in, reeled us in, reeled us in with your words about our splashing and kicking, how I washed Cookie's hair. Funny. Four of us squished into the tub. Funny."

She drew joyous reeling-in circles with her right hand and gripped an imaginary fishing pole in her left.

"Then you put that 'darkness' thing in there and you just dropped us? Like that? Right there you lost us."

"I dropped you? I should delete that line?" I asked.

With mind-bending aliveness and absolute confidence, she said, "Yup, it would be better. Way better."

She was right. Children know. They sense. They feel. May we bow to the true teachers. May this book help us listen to the kids and invite the adults to be learners. Life might be better. Way better.

Introduction

Children make your life important.
—Erma Bombeck

To Be a Grandparent

"I got this."

I fist-pumped when I first heard my first child was pregnant with her first babies, twins. To be a grandmother. Easy. I had changed hundreds of diapers for my six younger siblings, chased my two children around the circular neighborhood paths on their training wheel bikes, pushed their first two-wheelers until they steadied their balance enough to pedal on their own, launched them into adulthood when they steadied their life-balance enough to leave home, move out or get their first apartment.

I knew how to be a grandparent, I had four great ones, fine role models. Being grandma would be simple, like my certain truth that we succeed best when we cooperate. I would teach politeness. Non-violence. Please and thank you. I would help their inner beauty grow and young hearts blossom into wisdom and empathy. I'd teach them not to gloat when they hit a winning home run. I'd teach them not to spit on the ground, bat their arms, stomp legs and scream "No fair," when they'd sit on the bench. Winning and losing. Part of life. We'd learn to take turns with Chutes and Ladders.

I would come from "Yes, of course," not from, "No, no."

I would not shake my frown-faced head and point my straight, strict finger. They'd get enough of that in life.

I would promote social graces and model my Dad who was a champion golfer from Maine. When winning, Dad smiled, shook hands, congratulated the other players, the course management and the officials. "My competitors played well," or "I had some lucky breaks," or "Wow, that was tough competition."

Maybe more importantly, I'd let the kids know that gratitude also matters in moments of not winning (I wouldn't use the word losing). Dad again: "Congratulations. You played so well." or "You clearly outplayed me. You won fair and square."

His parents, my grandparents, taught him. I loved them, miss them, learned from them. Kindness and humility. I would be that kind of grandparent. No scolding, no lectures. Not me. I'm not that type. I read books, articles, and websites with titles like, *The Six Habits of Highly Compassionate People.*

I ask myself questions like, "How do I help deepen their Life Force?"

My grandkids would radiate this inherited goodness.

Then Life Happens

Bob & Fred 7 · Laudie 5

In a sunlit Florida-warm pool, coated with zinc oxide sunblock, playing a game that could be called Slam, Dunk, Hook, my vacationing twin grandsons, Bob and Fred, and a few of their friends jumped, threw balls, swam after them and splashed each other and their sisters in the turbulence of their cannonballs and belly flops until they didn't, until they huddled to taunt nearby girls:

Boys go to college to get more knowledge
Girls go to Jupiter to get more stupider.

My heart raced. My lips pursed. My eyes tightened. In that moment I did not care about the boys' vibrancy, nor their clear strength. I leapt from my poolside chair, pumped a fierce fist, and shrieked. "No! No!"

I shook my frown-faced head and pointed my straight, strict finger. "No! That is not okay. Stop! Stop it now!"

Mean, I unleashed fury.

Laudie and the girls gathered, hugged arms around each other's shoulders and faced the boys. They sing-songed:

Girls go to college to get more knowledge
Boys go to Jupiter to get more stupider.

I fell back into my bamboo chair, retracted my wagging finger, stopped yelling. I thought, "Maybe I haven't got this. Maybe I don't know how to be a grandparent. These girls know how to organize. They know how to take care of themselves. They figured this out without me."

Being grandparent comes with deep moral dilemmas, with doubts. Do we remind these precious little people, as I often do, about how others feel? Do we get out of the way; assume that their Life Force knows how to handle things? Do we stand up with both groups against name-calling and bullying? Is finger wagging and No-No ever okay?

What were those six habits of highly compassionate people? My father would know. What would Dad say?

Some grandparents simplify, "You get to have fun and then hand them over."

Naa. Being one generation removed from worrying about memorizing times-tables and flashcard homework, about not-throwing food and table manners is bigger than giving them back to their parents. Deeper. To have the long view from age seventy, to want and hope to say the right thing, and not to know what that is. To love them. To marvel at this infant coo, that toddler smile. And then the questions: How much time together? How often to show up? What to do when I don't agree with, oh, say, how much bacon they eat? How to be with them, with the family? What is my role as their mother's mother? I tell the you-get-to-send-them-home people, "Being grandparent is noticing what they teach about life's moments."

Contagious, children's happiness spreads. With their innocence in every new discovery, they entertain themselves and others. With their curiosity and wonder, they delight in the here and now: in the dawn, with hugs all day, and at sunsets. The wide-eyed ones, perhaps the greatest gurus, can train the older ones, who tend to fall asleep in the world. If we pay attention to their clapping, the little ones could teach the big ones how to write books with titles like, *Everything We Ever Learned About Joy, We Learned from the Grandchildren.*

I decided to write stories about how they spark their world alive, how they make magic. I wanted to capture their fears, sadnesses, joys. Mine too. This book is a crucible, a place where things and people change, morph, transform. Them and me. To be a grandparent, is to role-reverse and trust what we don't fully know, to be a student. Welcome to school.

My Family

Grandkids
as
Gurus

Beginner's Mind

In the beginner's mind there are many possibilities,
but in the expert's, there are few.
—*Suzuki Roshi*

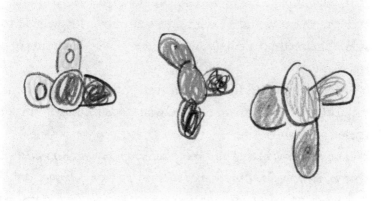

To Let Children Be Our Teachers

Bob & Fred 7• Laudie 5 • Cookie 3

I missed my grandkids. I missed their happy chaos. I ached to hear their wild voices. So, the day before my twin grandsons' seventh birthday, I called to video chat with all four siblings, for their guaranteed show and tell. Laudie appeared first. She had been scissoring into paper on the fold so that, when opened, a perfect square revealed itself (or whatever the shape would be with an exact mirror image side to side). She held up a cut-up white sheet, "Susu, look this one is a diamond."

Then she blurred the whole screen with another, this one tiny. "I have lots of them. Do you want to learn how to make these? I can show you."

I remembered taking paper napkins from my mother's kitchen drawer, right before dinner, and clipping pattern after pattern. I remembered the delight in the surprise in the unfolding, discovering what would pop as I unveiled the fullness of the form. At age five, I prided myself, as if a master artist, for inventing this nifty skill, "See, Mommy, see?"

With Laudie two states away with her piles of cut paper, I wondered, how do we lose that sense of our inborn genius? How do we forget what the Buddhists call the beauty of our true nature?

Cookie stepped into video chat next. She crawled onto the breakfast table, shot me a sly, shy yet radiant grin, and announced, "It's my birfday." It wasn't.

I thumbed-up at the joke. We giggled.

Our gaiety reminded me how spiritual teachers pose questions like, "When did you stop smiling? When did you stop laughing? When did you stop feeling joy?"

Many of us spend hours of adult years on yoga mats intending to regain that innate radiance. We raise our arms, inhaling to gather for ourselves huge Sun breaths and then exhale to shine Light to others. We fill our own cells then radiate lifeforce. We practice coming home to the inner brilliance we knew at two and a half.

Bob, one of the 6-year-olds-until-tomorrow, then displayed a hand-sized paper rocket. "It flies, Susu. Really, I'm not kidding."

In that moment with him, I let go of how I needed to scoot to the gym, then beat the crowd to Trader Joe's so I could check grocery shopping off my to-do list. I dropped planning mind, busy-brain, problem-solving and my ever-so-important busy-ness ahead. For kids there is no ahead. Bob and I shared a glimpse of pure presence, a space of refuge with no place to go just then, nothing to do, nothing to fix.

Then Fred, Bob's twin: "Susu, if you've lost anything, you should call me because I'm a great finder."

"Wow!" I said. "Please come here and help me."

Fred beamed. "I can. Someone lost something, and I found it. I didn't use my eyes or my ears. Nothing. I just knew where it was, and I went and got it."

"How did you know?" I asked.

"I just did. I told you. I'm good at that." No false bravado. No shame in claiming his triumph.

How do we later grow into dishonoring ourselves? Can we then return to our natural simplicity?

What if we saw such freshness in children not as naiveté but as vitality, so needed to sustain joy?

Imagine. What if....

To Grow Compassion

Bob & Fred 4 · Laudie 2 · Cookie 5 months

"Susu, they have a pool. And we'll eat popsicles. And they have cool ride-on trucks."

For days, my four-year-old twin grandsons Bob and Fred repeated their plans for a playdate at a friend's house. They had stuffed their backpacks with swimsuits and towels and sneaked in animal crackers to share. Then the friend's mom called to say she had strep throat and had to cancel. My daughter waited for tears or a tantrum from her sons. Instead, Fred said, "Oh, Mom. I hope she feels better."

Another time, when Fred spiked a fever and had to stay in bed rather than join the treasure hunt outside, he thought first of his twin brother playing without him, and said, "But I can't stay inside because Bob won't have fun if he's alone."

How, then, could light-filled Fred so cherish Tiki, his stuffed toy turtle? As he dropped off to sleep, Fred wrapped his hand around Tiki. Tiki, cute enough, with big round eyes and sparkly green skin, was filled with darkness. In Fred's palm, Tiki hit other stuffed animals and shrilled his voice into a sharp tone, "I win. You are *out*."

Tiki squeaked and woke up 4-year-old Laudie and 5-month-old Cookie.

On my next visit, I noted silence in the boys' bedroom. My eyes scanned the bed, the floor, the closet. Lego constructions with hundreds of pieces littered the plush carpet. Books filled shelves. Water bottles with Red Sox stickers leaked on the nightstand. "Hmm. Where's Tiki?"

Fred said, "Susu, Tiki was not kind. I tried to teach him to be nice. I sent him on vacation so he could take some time to be with himself. He's still pretty mean, but he's okay. He's learning."

In contrast, blabs my usual mind-rant, *My headache means I'm dying. Not only am I dying, it is my fault. Why am I suffering with sinusitis. If only I hadn't gorged on that pint of Phish Food, or maybe I didn't meditate enough last week. A donut and croissant for breakfast? And ice cream as lunch? What were you thinking?*

My husband tried to soothe, "That's pretty harsh."

I heard him, thanked him. Yet my pounding mea-culpa-ing yelled worst-case scenarios and blamed myself for them.

"I mean, you're not nice to yourself," he added.

Then I understood. I'd been hijacked by my inner Tiki. Under the spell of a Tiki-takeover, I could not be kind to myself. I stopped, listened, and cringed at the shrill finger-nails-on-a-blackboard of my inner Tiki attack. I couldn't hush Tiki's racket with my Tiki mind. I needed a force other than and bigger than "self." But I didn't know what until I heard the message taught by Fred, "You're okay. You're learning."

Ahhh. Deep inhale and exhale, and I quieted as if I'm in the boys' room with no Tiki. Then I sent myself a loving, "Oh, Susu, I hope you feel better."

On our own, we can't always let go of our unique form of human Tiki-talk. It took my husband to kickstart my forgiveness of the Ben and Jerry's lunch. Full healing came only through the light of a four-year-old.

To Speak Truth

Cookie 5

She hid when she greeted me, nestled between her mother's legs, avoiding eye contact. I held out my arms for a hug. She took two steps sideways, turned her eyes toward the garage door, glanced anywhere except at me, buried her face in her tiny hands. I made a bid for bonding, "Hey, Cookie, wow, that dress is so colorful. So soft and warm."

She looked down at her dress, a mix of pink and purple, patted its rainbow design. I said, "Fancy tights, too. I bet they're so fun to wear."

She corrected me, coolly, matter-of-factly, flatly, "They are not called tights."

I looked at her, "What are they?"

She looked at the driveway, started to draw on it with pastel chalk. I backed up several steps. After a few minutes, she tiptoed to me, rubbed her petite body against my legs. I bent and reached down, scooped her up, wrapped my arms around her as if holding her tight this once, right then, would assure we'd be tight forever. She melted into my arms. Both comfy now, her eyes met mine, a silent connection. She studied my face as if reading its features. She asked, "Susu, why do grandmothers have so many wrinkles?"

Kids say what they mean. We can count on them to be honest, at least at five, at least until the filters install themselves or are installed by grown-ups "(Shhh. We don't talk like that. We don't mention wrinkles")."

I said, "One day if you are lucky enough to be a grandmother, you will have wrinkles too."

She furrowed her brow, crinkled her nose, and shook her head, "Naaaah."

I nodded yes, raised my eyebrows, and smiled to highlight grandmotherhood as a good thing.

She touched my face. "It's all lines."

I said, "Uh-huh."

She added, "Kinda like prunes."

She was right. Kinda like prunes.

But adults don't talk truth like that.

To Know Feelings

Laudie 6 • Bob 9

"Bob is trying to own the Hoverboard. He thinks he can boss us around. He keeps telling me what I can do and what I can't do. That's the problem with having brothers. It's the worst!"

Laudie and I lay next to each other on her bed, because she had taken a dive off a hoverboard. She had skinned her now swollen and bloody ankle, and we had packed a plastic bag of ice on it. Tears dripped down her chapped red cheeks onto her achy shoulders. She used her mud-stained t-shirt sleeve to wipe both tears and dirt. A gang of kids squealed outside her window as they tested the new two-wheeled self-balancing scooter, given to the family as part of Bob's and Fred's ninth birthday celebration.

I tried to affirm her, "I see you are mad. You must've been so scared. And now you're sad."

She rolled away from me, tucking her body under her

11

mound of blankets, twisting them to cover even her glittery-painted toes, even her long blonde hair. She frowned and moaned, "Just so you know when I grow up, I will not, absolutely not, do the work my mom does with"—she mocked—"Social Eeeee-motional Learrrrrning."

She squinted and blah, blah, blahed her tone. "It's the worst. We even get it in school. I hate that part of second grade."

Fully knowing, I asked, "What is Social-Emotional Learning?"

She tugged at the bandage on her knee and said, "It's when teachers and parents help kids calm down, and we have to wait and be patient."

From his bedroom, taking a break from hoverboarding, third-grader Bob yelled, "Ya, we wait so long and have to be patient almost until a bomb hits."

Social-Emotional Learning asks more than the ability to be patient: it invites compassion, empathy, conflict resolution and problem-solving. Laudie had been clear: There would be none of it in my trying to help her soothe her post-fall physical wounds and younger-sister hurt.

After hearing "the worst" twice, I decided to offer Laudie some fun, "Let's play a game of worsts."

She smiled, "Yeah. Okay."

I asked, "What's the worst thing you can think of?"

She turned to me, unclenched her jaw, returned to normal

rather than staccato breathing, "Falling out of a tree."

I suggested, "Oh, how about we go by the alphabet?"

Rolling in to snuggle, she said, "Okay, what's the worst thing you can think of that begins with A?"

I said, "An airplane crashing. What's the worst thing you can think of that begins with B?"

She said, "Susu, there are only eight girls in my class and twelve boys. Boys!"

I cradled her and said, "Whoa, Boys!" Then I wondered, "Do you want to include what are the best things that begin with each letter?"

She said, "No, well, maybe, only after a few letters, so we have only some of the good stuff, but don't mess up our plan with the bad. Okay, what's the best thing that begins with C?"

"Hard C like K or soft C like S?"

She said, "K-K-K. Like K."

I asked, "You mean the best thing that starts with C like K?"

She said, "Yes,"

I yum-yummed, "Cookies, cake."

We reached F; my turn to ask, "What's the worst thing you can think of that begins with F?"

With no hesitation, she frowned, "Feeling lonely. Or fighting with friends."

Liking or hating social-emotional learning, that's how to know and speak true feelings.

To Give Consequences

Bob & Fred 9 • Laudie 7 • Cookie 4

"Come see what we found! You won't believe what we found!" Bob and Fred grabbed my elbow, and we sprinted to their bedroom.

Three drawers filled with UnderArmour soccer shorts, quick-dry athletic shirts and cotton pajamas lay stacked in a pile on their Lego-covered carpet. Rather than bureaus for storage, these drawers were built into the wall. Now the wall showed three gaping holes where the drawers had been removed. In that empty space, echoed the voices of Laudie and Cookie, from their bedroom down the hall.

"What?" I asked

The boys scrunched their bodies through the newly discovered, narrow alleyway between the two rooms. They inched through the crawlspace and pushed the back panel of the girls' closet, to surprise their younger sisters by popping into their bedroom.

Bob and Fred raised their arms in a victory V as do football players after a touchdown and chorused, "We found a secret passageway!"

Alone with them this night, their Mom and Dad out, I doubted the wisdom of their great find. I knew it wasn't safe. Were there rusty nails or dead or alive mice lurking in the dark there?

On the other hand, I remembered decades ago, the trips back and forth my five-year-old daughter and three-year-old son traveled in what seemed like a major highway to them under the eaves between their bedrooms in our first house. In the tiny white 1700s cape, we welcomed the extra play space. We had crowbarred the square doors off each opening and laid carpet samples on the rough, wooden floorboards to ease passage and to decorate. We added flashlights.

I told my grandchildren the story of their mom and uncle giggling in the same way, doing the same thing.

Yet I wondered, *Will their parents approve? Probably not.*

Was this a good idea? Probably not.

I let them laugh their way back and forth for a few trips, the boys discussing where else they could stash their pajamas, soccer shorts and quick-dry t-shirts to keep the drawers out of the wall permanently. The girls pushed aside their dresses to allow darting in and out of the closet—yet, to be clear—"Only when we want to."

But I needed them to end the frolic at bedtime. I texted their mom the big news with a picture, "You won't believe what they found."

She texted back, "Quiet time."

Yes, quiet time, moments to unwind the energy to ease into sleep. I reminded them in a soft hushed voice, "Quiet time."

They had heard this expression nightly for years, and would, of course, be ready, like me, for rest. Again with a smile, "Okay, guys, enough. Now it's quiet time."

They sneaked through the passageway; the boys roared "Boo!" each time they burst through the girls' trashed closet.

This time, the girls yelled, "No, stop!"

No one stopped.

I tried again but with just the teeniest bit more emphasis, as if I were Mom, as if that would help, and lilted, "Time to brush teeth."

As Bob and Fred dragged the drawers across their bedroom carpet, they screamed, "Susu, No! This is so fun!"

I raised my voice a smidge, "I know it's fun and how 'bout we read now?"

The girls shrieked, "Boys! We don't want you in our room."

The boys mimicked high-pitched voices, "But we don't mind if you're in ours."

I stared at them and lowered my voice, "What happened

to first time listening? Please, guys, we need to put the drawers back in the wall and get to bed."

But they were arguing, "My turn."

"No, my turn."

Confused and defeated, I opened my arms in the "Don't know" palms-up position, elevated my shoulders. "Guys, I'm having a hard time here. I asked you to stop, and you didn't. You had fun, and now it's time to settle down. I mean, stop. Come on! This is not fun for me."

They froze, stared back at me, then pointed their heads and eyes to the floor. Bob mumbled, "I only wanted to do one more thing."

Angry and firm, I said, "I know and No!"

Later I would tell their mom, "I had no idea what to do, felt powerless and ineffective."

The next week, before dinner Tuesday night, Laudie and Cookie dashed up the hill to the neighbor's backyard for zip-line fun with their friends. They pulled their helmets over their long blonde hair, strapped them under their chins, and started a civil turn-taking game. The zip-line scramble grew louder and louder, with four-year-old Cookie holding on longer, swinging back and forth—pushing the limits of her time.

Laudie said, "Come on, Cookie. Your turn is up. It's my turn now."

Ignoring her sister, Cookie bounced up and down.

Laudie begged, "Cookie, no fair. I'm going to take a longer turn, too."

Cookie held on, rode back and forth, zipped up and down.

My ears awakened when Laudie, said, "Okay, then, if you don't get down right now, I'm not going to talk to you tonight after lights out."

In mid-zip, Cookie jumped off the seat and handed it to Laudie.

I smiled to Laudie, as if to say, oh-that's-how-you-discipline.

She nodded, "yes."

Wednesday morning, Laudie, Cookie and I walked hand-in-hand to the basement to begin to stack sofa cushions into a hill, a tower. Cookie and Laudie would take turns. On our way down the stairs, I whispered to Laudie, "Yesterday I learned something from you. Remember last week, I could not get you to stop running under the eaves? I tried and asked nicely, and nothing worked? Then last night before dinner on the zip line, I watched you with Cookie. I heard you give her consequences! I could've used that. Brilliant! Thank you for that lesson."

Laudie smiled.

When we had pulled and deconstructed the cushions from the sofa, then stacked a pillow-pile to construct our mountain, Cookie climbed to the "summit," planted herself there crossing her arms over her chest. She bobbed her ponytails and flashed her mischievous "I'm not moving" look. Sitting cross-legged on the tile floor, Laudie raised her eyebrows to me, like a wink, like a "Watch this." She said, "Cookie, if you don't give me my turn, I won't talk to you tonight."

Cookie hopped down, snapped her fingers and said, "Here you go."

Laudie looked at me, smiled and nodded. I gave her a thumbs up.

To Feel Feelings

Bob & Fred 6 · Laudie 4 · Cookie 2

"Someday I wanna be taller than Bob," Fred lifted the top of his head, threw back his shoulders and pumped up his chest.

I wanted to talk with him, to explore the emotion behind I-wanna-be-taller.

I might have normalized it, "Me, too, sometimes I want to be taller."

Or I might have asked, "What's so great about being taller?"

Maybe I'd inquire, "Why?"

What was he feeling? Of course, I-wanna-be-taller might have been simply the need for 6-year old power. It might have been innocent, with no hidden meaning.

I blurted, "Maybe someday you will. You never know."

Looking at his barely-nibbled bagel, I almost said, "If you want to be taller, you have to eat more."

I didn't. Good thing. Fred hadn't asked for advice.

While I wondered whether wanna-be-taller was a feeling he had been carrying for the past few months and would live in him into the future, he moved into the present moment, "I gotta get dressed. It's soccer today. It's gonna be hot."

That's how we feel feelings. Note them. Accept them. Speak them. Do what needs doing. To be able to say, "Someday I want that. Today is this." Acknowledge and move on.

With it's-soccer-today, and my grandmother confusion about how to work with feelings, I remembered my doubts as a mother. How could I keep my fears about my wild son's outside-the-box creativity—his hilarious wit, his one-of-a-kind learning style—from squelching his brilliance? How could I let him know I was furious and yet be kind to him after he teased that girl about her underpants in second grade? Though I silently chuckled after he got kicked out of science class for dancing with the off-limits human skeleton, how could I make wanting to dance okay, yet help him tame the impulse to steal the skeleton from the closet? My emotions hurricaned until he left home. I had no role model then of "I gotta get dressed. It's soccer today. It's gonna be hot."

As a grandparent, I do some things right. I apologized to Laudie for starting our pre-bedtime reading of *The Wild Robot* without her. But later at home, the woulda-coulda-shoul-das erupted. I shoulda had the boys find her. I shoulda said

21

sorry to her for gathering without her. I talked to the boys about inclusion. But it was a lecture. I didn't help.

I did hug Fred as he cried, "Bob hit me. He's the worst brother in the world."

But I never circled back to Bob to address his part in their tussle.

And I forgot that feelings come and go, arise and pass, until Fred added, "And sometimes I really love him."

Feelings change so fast with the four of them: the happy hugs, the joy of climbing trees, the sadness of tears, the gladness of laughter, the pouting to get the mad out, the "I'm sorries" in forgiveness. One moment rolls by and then...and then a new one. Do I stay in this moment with them? "I see you're frustrated that you can't find your Under Armour shorts."

Do I go back into that last moment when Cookie demanded to sit with me at breakfast and I had said, "Oh, ugh, no. Fred and Laudie are sitting here."?

Their mom said, "Cookie, you are sitting across from Susu. You can see her really well."

Cookie made a two-year-old face as if to say, "Nice try," and then asserted for the third time, "I want to sit next to Susu."

How do we respond to a two-year-old's combination of mad-sad?

Being a grandparent is one of the best things in my life.

The burden of "I hope I didn't screw them up for life" is not on my shoulders. I am not holding big questions like, "Will they ever go to college? If they do, will I be able to afford it? Will they go to jail for some disciplinary infraction I never taught them to avoid? Do these kids still need a car seat?"

That background static in young parents who, at the same exhausting time, try to tame wild energy in toddlers and budding adolescents, is not generally present in grandparents. What I hold is an intention to hug, to laugh, to love and to be one of the people who lights up when they enter the room. Doubts arise, but the intention to love feels solid enough to hold the muddle of family life. Mostly.

And then. Fred, Bob, and Laudie strapped on their bike helmets (or were they ski helmets?) and scrambled up trees in their backyard.

"This is so fun, Susu. Watch."

I watched, heart in throat, teeth clenched. I didn't know what to do. I didn't want to broadcast my fear that they would crash to the earth. They climbed so high, pulling on each other's ankles and tugging on wobbly branches. Was fun worth the risk? I said, "Hey guys, I don't know what to say but...well... I know you love to climb. I love to climb too. But, I mean, is it safe? I love you so much that I don't want you to get hurt, and now here you are, all three in trees."

They shouted down to me, "Sure. Mommy and Daddy say it's fine."

They monkeyed from tree to tree, chattered like monkeys too, reached into each other's trees, shook the leaves to the ground.

Their mom yelled from the garage. "Time for school, guys. Come on out of your perches."

They climbed down. All three hugged me and said, "See, it was okay."

I said, "I was scared."

They said, "We get scared too. It's okay to feel afraid, Susu, and also to be brave."

To Ask Wise and Simple Questions

Bob & Fred 4

One night, after a splashy bath, some rugged wrestling, a jaunty argument over whose water bottle was whose, I tried to help Fred and Bob quiet their racing minds and still their jittery bodies. We read a quiet book. I slathered them with lavender body lotion. I tucked them in tight under their soft blue comforters. Then I started a CD, a child's version of a guided body scan. The velvety voice grounded them in an inner journey through the body, inviting them to notice and relax, moving from toes to head. As it started to direct deep breathing in and long, slow breathing out, the boys calmed. "Bring your attention to your toes," the kind man said. "How do they feel? Are they warm or cool? Can you feel the sheets against your skin? Can you take a deep breath and relax your toes?"

I heard the boys sigh, a big long exhale. *Ah*, I thought, *the boys are responding.*

The body scan progressed. Feet, ankles, shins, calves. I heard nothing from the usually rambunctious boys. *Ohhh, they are asleep or following along, letting go of tensions, part by part.*

I sneaked away from my silent and secret listening post behind their door. I fist-pumped, proud of my sleep hygiene intervention.

I tiptoed to the top of the stairs and heard Bob yell, "Susu, how do I let my knees drop through the earth?"

To Be Okay with Don't Know

Fred 5

"Oh my God," Fred would say.

When his parents heard him, they'd coax, "Fred, we don't talk like that."

They'd shake their heads, "No," or point their fingers, "Uh uh, Fred, do not say that."

But he did say that. His mom would say, "Fred, Stop."

He did not stop.

I decided to investigate. I asked, "Fred, do you know why not to say, 'Oh, my God?'"

He shrugged, "I don't know."

"Okay," I said, "Hmm. What do you know about God?"

Fred said, "I don't know about God. I know about Jesus."

I asked, "What do you know about Jesus?"

He said, "I don't know a lot. I do know how some bad guys tried to kill him by hanging him on something called a cross. But God is his father, and God made Jesus come alive again. And then something about someone, I'm not sure if it was Jesus or the bad guys, but someone lives in a castle. I don't know anything about the castle."

I wondered where to start. I proceeded without contradicting any story Fred might have heard. I said, "I saw a TV show about Jesus. What I know from that show is that Jesus was a man and teacher who taught about love and kindness. No one knows for sure whether he came back to life. I don't know about the castle. But maybe 'Oh my God' isn't so great because…what does it mean anyway? We don't know, right? Maybe we could come up with another expression like 'oh my goodness,' or 'oh my stars,' or 'oh wow.' Do you think it's just a habit to say, 'Oh my God?'"

He nodded, "Yes."

I offered, "Well then, let's practice another one over and over again, so then *that* will be your new habit."

He said, "Naaa, I'm okay."

Flash forward to Fred at five and a half. He hadn't practiced. When I'd hear him say, "Oh, my God," I'd counter, "Oh, my goodness."

He'd smile and say, "Oh, ya. I forgot. And Susu, well, now I know more, not all of the story, but more. Now I know Jesus was the good guy, and some other guys were bad. And I know the cross is true. But I still don't know about the castle. Now can we have a snack?"

To say, "I don't know" is a space to start. I could've gone on a treasure hunt researching a castle, or castles, or stories of castles or.... But I let his story be his story, which seemed fine to him and would open the possibility of his on-going discovery, his being free to grow into his answers. As if into a soft chair, we sank into the comfort of don't-know, sat, and ate some pretzels.

Joy

Find ecstasy in life; the mere sense of living is joy enough.
—Emily Dickinson

To Wake Up Happy

Bob & Fred 5 • Laudie 3

To stay in their rooms until the owl turns green. That was the rule. The owl: a type of child's clock. At night, after a wild bath, a wiggly storytime and rowdy snuggles, my grandkids checked that their toy owl's night-light shone orange. Its plastic face would turn green at the hour Mom and Dad set: Seven a.m.

When I visited, if I awoke in my basement guest room before seven, I closed my eyes and meditated, or stealthwrote in my journal, or checked e-mails on my tiny phone. But I did not get up. Ever.

I waited for the pitter-patter of toddler's feet, the twins' loud—barefoot, Laudie's muted by her pj's footies. First, I heard the din, two stories up as they trampled on the soft carpeted hall. I listened to their sparkle with which we are gifted at birth. The five-year-old boys and their three-year-old sister had not lost this gaiety.

Then they bumped down the runner on the stairway and hummed throughout the house. The three toddlers leaped down the next set of stairs onto the hardwood floor, nothing to muffle their steps, thundering, rumbling, roaring. They whispered to each other. "Shhhh. Tiptoe. Susu's sleeping. Let's surprise her."

Next in the tiled basement hallway, their giggly echoes reverberated with every footfall, with every "Shhh."

Clip-clop, clip-clop.

Then Bob, Fred and Laudie blasted into my bedroom. They smelled of last night's Burt's Bees Baby Shampoo and Kids' ACT Bubble Gum Fluoride Rinse. They shined ecstatic smiles at their "Let's-get-Susu" trick. Their delight radiated. They chorused, "Hi, Susu! The owl turned green! Time to wake up!"

With wide-eyed pretend amazement and a hint of faked disbelief, I stirred and groaned, "Mmmmm, you woke me up."

We hugged in the astonishment of those first moments. The morning rituals begun, I mumbled, "I have a great book here. How 'bout you hop into my bed and we read together?"

They coaxed, "Susu, get up!"

I strolled to the bathroom, scraped my tongue with my yellow plastic Ayurvedic tool trying to entice them, to slow them down, "Anyone want a turn?"

Fred did. He scraped and spit, then swished water and swallowed. Bob and Laudie said, "No! Come on!"

I reminded them, "No, thank you?"

At 7:05 a.m., they repeated, "No, thank you. Can we vroom our trucks or paint now?"

Squeezing my hand, they dragged me into the playroom. Possessed by cheer, they negotiated. Bob shouted, "Let's play with Legos."

Fred yelled, "No, I want to make a 'struction site with Lincoln Logs."

Laudie offered a new idea, and they bellowed a loud, "Yes! Let's build a pillow fort."

We threw apart the sofa to make "condominiums." Bob and Laudie wanted big ones, with connectors between them so that they could pop in on each other. Fred demanded a teeny cozy one with a rooftop outlook for Scooby, his stuffed toy turtle. Seat cushions made walls; back cushions became roofs. The siblings sneaked from "room" to "room," rearranging the "doors." They jumped up and down, burrowed through openings. Bob flipped, somersaulted, bolted out of our construction site and skipped back with my bed pillows. "I need these. My 'margination told me to create a skyscraper."

They then decided to mess up the bolsters enough to make a pit. They hoisted themselves onto the window wells above, scurried across the white windowsills and plopped onto the bouncy landing with warrior glee: "Kowabunga" or "I win!"

At seven-ten in the morning.

At home in Maine, the day dawns lazier, my sinking into a leisurely meditation or savoring a quiet bowl of oatmeal while I puzzle through the Jumble in the newspaper. Whether charming light-bearers awaken us or whether we roll out of bed with our own enthusiasm or lethargy, perhaps we can greet the sunrise enchanted. Maybe as adults we could benefit by the excitement of a clock that turns green, even if only in our early morning consciousness. With or without spirited toddlers, what if we met the morning with such a boost of bliss?

To Delight in Delight

Bob & Fred 9 · Laudie 7 · Cookie 4

I had started to read *The Book of Delights* by Ross Gay, in which he wrote for a year a daily delight journal, recording joys. I decided to adopt that practice, to banish depressive thoughts, to focus on the pleasant in this not-always-pleasant world, to open my eyes and ears.

The first day I wrote about how this writing would remind me of the 13th-century Persian mystical poet Rumi's quote, "There are hundreds of ways to kneel and kiss the ground," granting permission to love the world however we love.

He also wrote, "Let the beauty we love be what we do."

Yes, I'm in.

Day two: I saw only brokenness in politics, in poverty, in the opioid epidemic, and in climate change.

The third day it rained, and I found only gray and mud.

The fourth day I realized that awakening to wonder would

require looking, feeling, seeing, whatever appeared in front of me. It didn't have to be big.

Day five, I wrote about the old, used kiddy buggy we bought at the local transfer station for the grandkids. It had been a deal at two dollars, a deal which kept them occupied for hours a day over weeks, patching it together with neon orange duct tape, decorating it with frayed ropes and the foam insides of moldy pillows, finding ways to make it turn when the worn plastic tires wouldn't.

Still, I struggled with the writing-delight practice.

On day six, I video-chatted with four-year-old Cookie. Her voice lilting, she said, "Susu, did you know I can ride a bike?"

My heart swelled. I said, "Wow, a bike?"

My body, my bones, felt what Ross Gay called his "delight radar."

Cookie beamed, "Ya, do you want to know what I can do on a bike?"

I beamed back, "Sure."

"Well, first," she pointed 'one,' "it's a big kid's bike, no training wheels. I can ride a two-wheeler."

I said what one says when one is full of delight, "Wow!"

"And I know how to stop it. You know, Susu, you can't go backwards on a bike."

"No?" I asked.

"No. But I can pedal backwards."

"What happens if you pedal backward?"

"Susu, don't you know? If I pedal backwards, that stops the bike. You didn't know that? It's called braking."

I said, "Seriously? Braking? So interesting."

She stood. "At first I had trouble with that. I lost balance, but now—akch'lly—I can pedal backwards without falling off. "

"Cookie! You can pedal backward without falling off? Amazing."

Cookie jumped to demonstrate, "I can also go around corners."

I asked, "How do you turn a bike around a corner?"

She said, "You don't turn the bike. Handlebars don't turn."

I chuckled. "Oh. Handlebars? They don't? Then, how do you go around corners?"

"You lean." She showed me, almost tipped over. "See? Like this."

"Oh! I see."

"And I can go uphill and downhill and those take different things to do."

"Ya? Like what?"

"Well, going up is hard and I have to pedal kinda like stronger and coming down I have to—well, sometimes I take my feet off the pedals coming down."

"Is that dangerous?" I asked.

With her four-year-old bravado, she fairly sang, "Not for me."

She smiled. I clapped. Then I knew how to write that delight practice.

To Persevere

Bob & Fred 3

"Vroom. Vroom. Vroom."

Fred and Bob paraded their newest metal toy, echoing its motor sounds throughout the wide expanse of their spacious dining and living room. They wound up a way-too-noisy yellow dump truck, fingernail-screeching it on the wooden table until it plopped and crashed on the bare, oak floor, smashing some leftover spilled Cheerios in the landing spot. They giggled, climbing over each other again and again for the entire journey of the rattling Tonka. Then, eyes twinkling, they raced to grab the truck yelling, "Dump truck crash."

They perched the truck on the table and pressed the button. "Go!"

Each time their little machine landed on the floor, they laughed and hopped up and down, "more crash," or "dump truck crash again."

I worried about the wrecking ball quality of this play. I

said to the kids, "Let's move to a quieter room, maybe the playroom. We could play in the carpeted hushed basement, with its sound-absorbent drapes."

But Fred and Bob ran and jumped and took turns and laughed, and ran and jumped and took turns and laughed, and ran. They rolled over each other, in a toddler wrestling match, hundreds of times, to get to that button. "Crash again." "Dump truck crash." "More crash."

And they clapped.

They teach presence, I said to myself. *They inhabit here, now, every moment a chance to have fun.*

I said to my husband, "Hey, Papa, maybe they are learning the gravity game. The truck falls off the table every time. Yup, down it goes again."

We laughed with the boys, even as we remembered their mom's words to us yesterday, "Mother, Father, this is not a behavior I want to reinforce. This is not sustainable."

Yes, these are her children who will live in this house long after we leave. My daughter was right, of course, And yet these boys showed perseverance—as furniture damaging as it was. They taught us some things about playing just for the fun of it.

Later that day—a day with no wind, no breeze, a still, heavy summer day—we loaded up a red Radio Flyer wagon with animal graham crackers, water bottles, changes of shorts and t-shirts, and a kite with a multi-colored tail. We trekked on the cement sidewalk to a neighborhood park. The boys took turns vrooming the kite string around the parched baseball diamond, throwing it high, dropping it, picking it up again. Fred zigged; Bob zagged. Fred then bounded to the kid-size slide and climbed to its top to boost the height of the kite. Down it crashed. Bob scrunched the collapsed rainbow-colored nylon from the dry ground and marched off again. Apparently, these silly kids didn't know the kite didn't work that day—or they didn't know the "supposed to" rule about kites. They laughed and chased the tail and leapt over the string for forty minutes (I counted). My husband and I yelled to the kite, "Up, up."

They imitated, "Up, up."

Forty minutes. With no idea that the kite was failing. They pushed through, long after I would have meandered home. They filled their lungs and sprinted, long after my grandmotherly breath said, "Enough."

This is perseverance.

To Play

Bob & Fred 2

I wondered about the clip-clopping. My daughter said, "The boys are fascinated by shoes, my shoes, their dad's shoes. They're bombing around the house dragging shoes, putting huge shoes on their tiny feet. Clomp. Clomp. Clomp."

To support their fascination, I decided to write something about shoes and then share it with them. I wanted what I'd create to add fun for them, for me, for us.

I went to work, humming. I would craft a book. They would love this, just the right thing. I cut out pictures of brown work boots, black high heels, white tennis shoes and one of a woman's leg draped over a bathtub sporting a strappy sandal. I wanted the two-year-old twins to guess about the shoes on each page. Would these be Mommy's heels, Daddy's loafers or their new toddler boots?

I imagined they would prize my clever work; hold this book dear among others. We would sit in a calm, maybe dimly lit room, snuggled together and cuddled under a warm blanket. We'd read and laugh. I'd hug them. Or they'd jump into bed with me, one twin on each side. We'd turn the pages and play the guessing game. It would be dreamy.

I held the book, stroked its laminated pages, patted my thighs to invite them up to read. They resisted, "No, no, that's not the book I want. Susu, I want *this book* instead."

They slapped the board book, *Eight Silly Monkeys*, into my palms.

Even as the oldest of seven children in a busy family, even as the mom in a chaotic two-child family, even after so many experiences of kids wanting one thing and my mind imagining another, still, I held onto the vision of us pointing to the Adidas, the Nikes, New Balance, all the pictures I had pasted then organized and collated.

When I pushed, "Come on, let's look at shoes," the two-year-olds ran to get their Velcro-fastening sneakers, put them in their mouths, chewed the rubber soles, then rounded up Daddy's loafers, slipped them on and clomped around the house in them. They giggled, frolicked, and rolled over each other. They delighted in the non-reading, the non-book. My happiness, of course, depended on the degree to which I could let go of expectations, of my lesson plans, and to allow myself to follow the silly monkeys on the page and the two silly monkeys on my lap.

To Celebrate

In these moments, nothing else mattered. Bob and Fred simply turned the colorful cardboard pages of their toddler board books. They lifted their gaze now and then, looked up at the adults sitting with them. They clapped when they saw a brightly spotted black and white image of a cow in the book. Simple. They said, "Mooooo."

Then they danced and bounced their heads to the song, "If you're happy and you know it, clap your hands."

They stopped after a verse here and there to bring their palms together and beam genuine entire-face smiles, eyes crinkly at the edges. Just this. Engaged.

I thought, "These boys know how to party. This is serious play."

I remembered Nietzsche's words that our maturity consists of "having rediscovered the seriousness that (we) had as a child at play."

Bob's winsome sapphire eyes teased. Fred's magical grin lured me into the hundred and tenth round of "Head and shoulders, knees and toes (knees and toes). Head and shoulders knees and toes."

The boys giggled. As soon as the lilting tune started, "Head and...." their chubby hands popped up and slapped the sides of their temples. They raised their eyebrows, Fred's dark, Bob's blond. Like schoolchildren making sure the teacher spots them, the twins called out, "See? See?"

Their mother, father and grandparents exclaimed, "We see you. Yes, that *is* your head. *Yaaay!*"

Their fingers twirled strands of hair, yellow and brown, and then they clapped. They cavorted a bit and laughed a lot.

Bob knew other body parts, so the adults prompted him, "Where's Bob's tummy?"

He patted himself, like a jolly Santa's ho-ho-ho. "Yeaaaaah."

Bob led the applause. I clapped, too, and tickled his belly.

Fred's spindly legs, newly walking, now skated over the carpet. He sprinted to the middle of the room, his face brightened, and eyebrows lifted as he spotted everyone watching him. Staring at his adoring fans, mid-run, he braked to a standstill. He stopped, clapped, then changed direction and jogged toward the windows where he watched the passing Golden Retriever, clapped again and woof-woofed back across the room.

Bob grunted "Uh-uh," perhaps code for "Watch me!"

The adults asked, "Bob, what does a fish say?"

He scrunched his mouth open and closed, his tightened lips, poofed them out and then pulled them in. Bob pushed himself up from a crawl onto two legs, clapped at the top, dipped and squatted a few times, clapped again. His round baby blues invited us to join him in his standing ovation.

To Love

Bob 2

Cradled in his mom's lap, Bob called to video chat. Eyes shining, he smiled and reached both arms up through space to hug me. He covered his eyes, laughed as he opened his tiny hands and beamed, "Peek-a-boo."

He asked me, "Susu, you coming? Susu come in car with me?"

He pursed his lips to kiss the screen and waved, "I wuv you," before he pushed the button to disconnect.

This is the love of a two-year-old. May we remember to experience it fully, purely, daily.

To Trust What You Know

"Do I change out of my pajamas now and into play clothes? What do you think, Susu?" asked Cookie one morning, deciding whether or not to get dressed.

I wore black yoga pants and a gray hoodie. She pulled purple and pink striped leggings out of her drawer, and rolled out a flowered shirt for the top, also purple and pink. Then she threw them on the floor in a pile which looked like a fashion volcano crisis had erupted, with other tops, pants and skirts. She shuffled in her drawer for this t-shirt, then unearthed that long-sleeved shirt, then demanded this sweater. She wasn't sure if she wanted tights, shorts or pants. No more piles now; her clothes were scattered. They covered the creamy carpet.

She justified her choices, "This striped one matches that plaid one because they're both pink and purple. See? This sweater goes under that t-shirt because it feels better against

49

my skin." She pulled out cotton underwear on which the elastic rim said, "Wednesday."

I said, "Tomorrow is Wednesday. Today maybe you want to wear Tuesday's undies."

"Naaaa, I like these because I like the pink band around the top."

My adult brain had been hijacked by what's right and what's wrong in the eyes of those who sell clothes. Cookie, not caught by marketers, knew what she knew and knew what she liked. She pulled on her final answer of pink and purple striped tights, a pink and white tutu, a soft long-sleeved sweater layered with a white t-shirt with a big glittery heart on it ("so the heart will show").

She asked, "Are you going home today?"

"Yes."

"Well, Susu," she pondered as she looked over my black yoga pants and gray sweatshirt. "Why are you wearing what people wear to the gym?"

Fair question. "Because these clothes are baggy and comfy and roomy."

She had her standards. "But you're going on a plane. Why are you wearing sweaty pants?"

To Let Go

Laudie 4

Laudie said, "You should dress 'kinda fancy' for the tea today at my preschool."

I asked, "What does 'kinda fancy' mean?"

She said, "Susu, did you know my favorite colors are pink and ..."

She pointed her index finger in the air and slowed down, "*Blue!*"

I asked, "Whoa, *blue*? What happened to purple?"

She answered, "I used to like purple, but it's too dark. I like light colors. Are you going to wear bwight colors?"

I said, "I have sort-of fancy pants and a kind of fancy sweater but they're blue and white."

"Like this color blue?" she asked, pointing to the aqua on the toe part of her sock.

I hoisted my leg to show her the navy stripe on my pjs. "No," I told her, "more like this."

"Well, it'll be okay. I am going to wear this, I think."

From a pile on her floor—was it clean or dirty laundry? I didn't know—she grabbed a pale-pink, sleeveless dress, pulled it over her head, ripped it off and threw it back on the floor. I asked her, "Won't you need tights for your legs. It might be co....."

Before I could finish, she pulled a brand-new-looking, larger-sized, rainbow-colored and deep-pink dress from her closet. It too was sleeveless and I said, "Hmm. So bright. So many splotches of shiny colors. I wonder how cold you might be this misty, damp spring day. The colors match so well. It seems so comfortable."

She seized a lighter, pastel-pink sweatshirt—the one with hearts—out of my hands as I started to toss it into the washing machine, "Susu, I'm going to wear that to the tea."

Maybe her dress was Lilly Pulitzer—it was that beautiful. With the fancy dress on, she threw her mud-covered, chocolate-stained well-loved not-laundered oversized sweatshirt over her bare arms, then pulled on mismatched ankle socks and well-worn sneakers.

"Now I'm dressed. I got myself dressed all by myself. Now can we go climb on the play set? Do you wanna see how I can climb?"

"Sure."

With bare legs she slid down the cold metal fireman's

pole. She said, "Do you wanna know what we're gonna to do?"

Not sure if she meant what tricks we're gonna do next as a gymnast or later that day, I said, "Of course."

In her choice of fashion for the tea, she was upside down trying to fit her feet into a rope-attached bucket too small for them. She wanted me to give her a ride in it. She chatted, "Well, when you come in, you don't just come in. I will meet you at the door and take you to your seat. Then you don't wait on me. I wait on you. You can have lemonade if you want and there'll be a menu so you could have tea, too, if you want. Anything you want."

I arrived fifteen minutes early since I wasn't sure of the exact protocol for preschool teas, and sat in the parking lot with other "guests" until I saw Laudie's neighbor walking up the path toward the entrance, dressed in a full-length dressy dress with party-worthy jewelry. Her simple black dress was beautiful as she entered the classroom, escorted by her pink-bowed, patent-leathered-shoed daughter.

Then Laudie bowed her head, smiled and sauntered—no doubt in Montessori style. She squeezed my hand and led me to the same teeny table where her friends sat. The students had made name placards. My name was all in caps, SUSU, with a little curly-Q at the bottom of the U. If the letter had been closed at the top, you might have thought it a Q.

The room was strewn with kid-made construction-paper strips hanging from the ceiling, tables decorated with homemade placemats and napkins. Moms and dads filled the space, kids dragging them from paint stations to quiet carpets for reading time.

Menus, printed by the three- and four-year-olds: fruit kabobs, cucumber sandwiches, tarts, lemonade, mint tea. Each place had a napkin held by a napkin ring, edged with stamps, and a single seashell next to each plate. "We set the table like this," Laudie puffed up as she told us.

Laudie grinned and took our orders, then hustled, business-like, to the happy chattery serving area. As if a waitress, she carried tiny, finger food to me. Laudie poured lemonade for herself. "Way too sour," she said.

She jumped up from her child-size seat and marched back for mint tea. "You can have this little mint here—like this is how we put it on the plate next to the cup—if you want, Susu, but I don't like it so do you want it or not?"

We finished eating. I had a fruit kabob. While sipping our drinks, I told Laudie, "My mint tea is *perfect*."

The teacher crossed her hands over her heart to signal "Shhhh" and led the students to sit in a circle on their meeting rug. They sang a song that they had been practicing for the event. Something like "My Name is Us," with its beautiful message of inclusivity, a tear-jerker. I stood in the back, facing Laudie sitting amid her friends cross-legged on the edge of the carpet. To the other mothers, I said, "I always cry at these things."

The tea lasted about an hour. At the end, I leaned into Laudie to say, "Thank you for inviting me. I love you."

After such sweet connection, Laudie sat on my lap, her arms around me. I reached to give her a good-bye hug, hoping she would let me go, hoping it would be okay with her that I leave.

She didn't notice. She said, "I'm going outside, Susu, Bye."

In one hand she carried a little plant ("I planted that myself," she had told me earlier). Her other hand entwined with a friend's, she filed outdoors. Skipping to the playground, she never turned back to wave.

To Love in All Colors

Laudie 7 · Cookie 4

Veggies. Fruits. Green smoothies. Dried goji berries. For Saturday lunch, like a mature adult, like a good grandmother, and because of nutritional Jiminy Cricket, I plated healthy food for Laudie and Cookie, visiting in Maine from their home near Boston.

I arranged scrumptious strawberries, purplish grapes, organic blueberries, raspberries, blackberries, cut-up cantaloupe and honeydew. Around the edges, I decorated as an artist would—since Laudie self-identifies as artist—with carrots, yellow and red peppers, green celery, darker broccoli.

I ta-daahed my platter, sashayed its loveliness to the goldenrod-hued table and said to my granddaughters, "Look! A kaleidoscope of colors. It's good to eat the rainbow every day, you know?"

Laudie paused, flashed her menacing and marvelous smile, shook her head no, and stated, "Ak'ch'lly, I like brown."

I chuckled. We chuckled together. I asked, "Ya? Like what?"

Her face widened, her voice lilted, "like chocolate milk, waffles, pancakes, cookies."

I wondered to myself, *When do brown cravings start?*

I recalled a 1950s Easter.

The eternity of two days had passed in which my brother Mike had not yet eaten his chocolate bunny. I was maybe eleven, he four. How did he let that brown, Russell Stover goodie sit so long in the fridge? I had devoured mine by Sunday noon: Tuesday, I sneaked into Mike's, sucked off the two stuck-together ears. Wednesday, I gnawed away the head.

I also love brown. I get Laudie.

Browns in the 50s? Lunch: Skippy or Jif Peanut butter. Dinner: Hamburgers. Friday night: Fish sticks and French fries. Saturdays: B&M baked beans and brown bread. Dessert: Betty Crocker Double Chocolate Chunk Cookies; Friendly's coffee ice cream with Hershey's fudge sauce; Sarah Lee Brownies. I remembered liking brown but didn't tell Laudie. No need to fuel her preference.

That weekend Laudie and Cookie crawled through forts they built with sofa cushions. They designed, then hurdled over barriers in an obstacle course engineered from basement-dwelling, dust-gathering gym equipment. We frolicked and porpoised up and down in an indoor pool. They poured brown snacks (sesame sticks and cashews) for Molly and Kirsten, their mom's American Girl dolls. We cuddled to cheer the Celtics on TV. Laudie tried to teach Cookie to twist a fidget-spinner around her too-tiny fingers. We giggled over made-up knock-knock jokes. I played "ice cream shop customer," ordered pretend soft-serve, and paid with marbles. We curled up as they listened to me read *Love You Forever*. They joined in when I read the chorus.

I cry with that book. I never had dry eyes with my own children and didn't with my daughter's daughters. The message of never-fading compassion seems poignant—no, crucial—now. Care-full ideas. Kind-full themes. Tears came. Cookie and Laudie stared, "Crying? Why are you crying? This book is about love!"

I said, "Love is *why* I'm crying."

They squinted and said, "Now can we have those brown Junior Mints you hid? Those are about love too."

For dinner I cut new fruit and veggie shapes, plated a spiffy pattern and said, "Here you go, luscious colors, today's rainbow."

Cookie scrunched her nose. Laudie sparked her sly smile, "Naa. I'm having a brown day."

I'll love them forever. I'll like them for always....

To Adventure

Laudie 7

"I call this the eyeball path," Laudie said. "It's round and big. See how my eyeballs go down on the bottom and then up around, like this path?"

On the Friday before Mother's Day, hiking in the Berkshires, Laudie with her long legs and I with my short ones hopped logs and dodged mud. We had just climbed out of my Subaru after a two-hour drive over the springtime mountains. This trip to a retreat center for 'Yoga and Art for Kids' was a birthday gift to my granddaughter.

As we tromped along, I snapped pictures of her to send to her parents who lived near Boston. She sniffled, "Can we Facetime Mommy and Daddy?"

"Sure," I said.

She covered her face with her thin fingers and tightened her lips to resist a frown, "My eyes are watery."

When her mom appeared on the screen, Laudie fake-smiled into my phone. Her mom noted her expression and asked, "You okay?"

Laudie nodded. Her mom's gaze found mine. My look said, "Right now is hard." I mouthed, "Homesick."

After the call, I knelt to meet Laudie eye-to-eye, and said, "I'll stay with you as long as you want. You'll never have to look for me. This whole weekend I'll be with you or nearby."

We later went to dinner. Beyond the vegetarian and the non-vegetarian cafeteria lines, we spotted a family with a young girl, whose nametag spelled Lora. Laudie pointed to her, "Let's sit there."

We joined them. Laudie and Lora whispered, giggled, chatted, and then wondered, "Is this a program we're doing? Camp? Class? What do we call it?"

7:00 p.m. At session one, orientation, with twenty-six children ages five to twelve, I asked one of the seven teachers, "May I stay?"

"Of course," answered the leader.

After playing initial get-to-know-you games, Lora, 9, and Laudie, decided together, "This is boring."

They rolled out their yoga mats next to each other. They debated whether to swap water bottles.

I asked Laudie, "Is it okay if I leave for just a bit to go unpack?"

She squiggled closer to Lora's mat and, flipped a care-free hand, "Sure."

I asked, "Do you want me to come back after I unpack, check in on you, or see you at the end?"

She glanced at smiling Lora. They hooked arms and Laudie waved me off, "...just at the end."

As I turned to leave, Lora's six-year-old brother stopped me and lifted a pile of stapled paper to my face. "I made this book. It's called, 'Emotions.'"

We sat together on a mat and turned the pages; each page named an emotion and had a related drawing. Happy. Sad. Angry. Scared. Lost.

I said, "Awesome. Everyone has feelings like scared, lost, mad, sad, or glad."

Wanting Laudie to see the "lost" page, I found her next to Lora, both balancing on yoga blocks. I pointed out the sketch and said, "You know how we felt lost at first... how we had trouble finding our way?"

She shook her head no, "I wasn't lost."

I reminded, "How we weren't sure where that eyeball path led, then your eyes watered?"

Her arm swished, "Oh, ya. I forgot."

I said, "You can remember this next time you go adventuring. How feelings change. How you felt one way to start and then a new way later. You can trust yourself on adventures to make friends and get comfortable with what was uncomfortable."

She squinted, "Mmm," then turned to Lora to ask, "Do you know how to play the bubblegum game?"

At lunch on the last day of what Lora and Laudie settled on calling, "the program," in a clattering dining room, we video-chatted with Laudie's mom. It was Mother's Day after all. "I love you SOOO much," her mom said.

Laudie said, "I can't hear you. Bye."

She clicked the red circle on my phone to end the call, handed me my phone and turned to Lora to sing-song, "Bubblegum, bubblegum in a dish. How many pieces do you wish?..."

Adventures are like that.

To Have Big Gratitude for Small Favors

Fred 8

My daughter's neighbor, Mrs. D, arrived in the driveway with her own children in her van to pick up my same-age grandkids for school. As she herded them, she saw her son Donny's green bike in my daughter's driveway. Mrs. D smiled, "Oh, pffft. Leave it there. I'll come get it later."

I pulled it up closer to the garage door to get it out of the way.

Later as Fred hopped out of the car, after school. I said, "Fred, should we move that bike?"

He asked, "Is that my bike?"

I said, "I don't know."

Without looking at it or me, busy pulling on his rain boots so he could race, scooter and bike-ride through puddles and mud, he pointed to the air, "They're akch'lly exactly the same except for the bell. Look at it. Does it have a bell?"

Grabbing a chocolate protein bar for him from the stacked shelves of the snack cabinet, I squinted from the kitchen door. I couldn't see tiny bell detail.

He said, "Oh. Nope, not mine. I'll ride it over there."

Fully helmeted, Fred pedaled standing on his friend's bike. With one hand on the handlebars, he twisted his wiry body halfway off the seat, waved to me with the other arm and yelled as he streaked away, "I'm going to Donny's. He's my best friend. I'll be right back. It's okay. Mommy and Daddy let me go by myself."

I was not sure of that. Not sure he'd stop and look three ways at the crossroad. I started to yell, "Safety first, Fred. Check for safety."

Too late: he'd flown off. He swooped back on his own bike about fifteen minutes later.

"Susu, look at my bike. It is so clean. Those cleaning people over there are *SOOO* nice. They washed my bike."

I asked, "Was the family home?"

"Nope, just the cleaning people and they are *soooo* nice. Look at my bike, Susu. It is *SOOO* clean! I remembered to say 'thank you.'"

To Laugh About Silly Things

Laudie wore swim goggles in the tub, her "sundasses," during and after the bath, bobbing her head under the water, popping up reporting, "I swim, Susu. I swim."

I laughed. She laughed. Her four-year-old twin brothers Fred and Bob laughed. After my three grandchildren had finished playtime in the tub, they snuggled into their robe-like towels. All three asked me for what they called my "magic sleeping lotion" which I had brought from Maine, a tiny tub of Badger's Nighty-Night Chamomile and Bergamot paste that they smeared over their bath-reddened cheeks, saying, "Mmmmm. Susu, smell me."

I sniffed them. They smelled of baby Orajel training toothpaste, Johnson's Baby Shampoo. And Magic Sleep lotion. With a warm heart, I smiled.

I put Laudie in her crib in her nursery, then sat with the twins in their bedroom's pillowed reading nook. We read

Thomas the Train and *Mr. Magee Goes Camping* twice each. We played the end-of-the-day game: "My favorite part of the day is..."

Fred volunteered first, "My favorite part of the day was hiding in the car when Daddy was about to give Susu a ride and I said, 'Boo.'"

Bob's favorite part of his day was, "Playing with Fred, chasing each other in the backyard."

We hugged and kissed. I turned the lights out, closed the door just the right amount, which demanded rugged negotiating, and—exhausted—trudged downstairs to put dinner dishes away, fold laundry and organize stacks of wooden blocks. Maybe I'd relax now and boil a big cup of hot water for tea.

I heard Fred and Bob partying, jumping on their beds, laughing. I sneaked to their door to listen. Fred squealed, "Here, you take Turtle."

He threw it to his brother. Bob said, "Okay. You take Bunny," and tossed it.

They rolled around, out of their beds, on the floor giggling. I heard Laudie cry, "Me, me." She whined, "I want to be with the boys."

I heard the boys chucking blankets, ditching toys and unwrapping sheets from around them. What to do? Get Laudie? Pick her up? While I wondered how to handle the rowdy boys, I also questioned the best way to care for Laudie. Do I leave her alone and let her practice her self-soothing sleep routine? Will she ever drift off? Can we do grandparenting wrong?

In an attempt to model shhhhh and nighty-night, I tip-toed into the boys' room and whispered, forefinger to my lips, stifling a laugh at the pile of stuffed animals strewn over their carpet. "Hey, guys, it's time to get in your beds. It's time to go to sleep."

Fred patted my back, "Susu, it's okay. We're just talkin' 'bout silly things."

Sometimes I long for linear: If they say this, then I'll say that. If they do A, then I'll do B. But this time I followed the crooked way. With no straight-line intervention, I let Laudie be (she was now singing). With perhaps less discipline than prudent, I let the boys be and I laughed 'bout silly things.

Kindness

And you can always, always, give something, even if it is only kindness.
—Anne Frank

To Know When We Need Help

Bob & Fred 6 • Laudie 4 • Cookie 2

One Friday night, a babysitter made sure Cookie brushed her teeth and spit out the toothpaste. This college student supervised a bubble bath, and helped Cookie change into her pink-striped pajamas as Cookie's mom washed and dried dinner dishes. She read *Good Night Moon* three times, handed Cookie her lovies, tucked her in, and said, "Good night. See you tomorrow. I'm leaving."

Cookie insisted, "You can't leave. I need a gwown-up in here."

Later that week, I played with Cookie in a shallow pool for toddlers. I pulled and pushed her on a kickboard, fetched the yellow foam noodle each time it popped off her belly, and taught her how to dive for rubber dinosaurs at the bottom by diving for rubber dinosaurs at the bottom. We frolicked for about an hour, then my grandmotherly energy tanked. I said, "Susu's tired. I'll go sit on the edge and take care of you from there."

Cookie sobbed, "No! I need a gwown up in here with me."

Cookie knew that a child needs an adult, not a hovering, judgmental, tough type or a laissez-faire-not-even-watching type, but a grown up. She knew that the grownup should be present, should pay attention. "I need a gwown up here." Clear.

On Sunday, we loaded a van for a multigenerational road trip. Two grandparents, two parents, four children. We packed books for them. We remembered to give them their stuffed animals to hold (or to throw at each other, it turned out). We doled out paper and crayons for drawing. Yet we forgot to lock the van's windows. Soon the children burst into giggles with their game of windows buzzing up and whizzing down from both sides of the back seat. Distracted from driving, their Dad said, "Okay, kids. Enough. Safety first."

Creating order, setting limits, making ground rules, takes a grown up.

We drove to a farm which featured an ice cream stand. My four grandchildren scattered. One bolted across mud to see the cows. One followed the cute bunnies and almost vanished. The other two climbed wet walls and forbidden fences. Their parents herded all four and led them to the ice cream window. Bob said, "I want the biggest cookies and crème cone, three scoops."

His mom knelt beside him, held his hand, looked into his

round eyes and whispered, "Can I help you with this? I'd like to invite you to make a different choice."

Bob said, "Okay."

I remembered my own refrain from childhood. "I scream. You scream. We all scream for ice cream. Give me a huge, chocolate-chip, cookie-dough on a sugar cone, with M&M mix-ins, and rainbow sprinkles."

I watched my mind and its I-scream craving. Even as an adult on this day at the ice cream stand, I, too, wanted the biggest until I heard a grown-up echo in my head, "Can I help you with this?"

What if, as we age, we could become friends with our interior big people, the ones able to craft wise decisions for us? What if our mature parts cozied up, made eye contact and held hands with the parts that act like six-year-olds? Maybe, like Bob and Cookie, we could accept guidance from our ever-present inner gwownups as they lead us to order and safety, and invite us to "make different choices."

And we could say, "Okay."

To Walk up to Fear to Touch It
and to be All-Done-Scared

Fred 3

Fred said, "I reading to truck."

He turned page after page mumbling three-year-old gibberish, pointing out pictures to the truck in his hand.

Later came this text from his mom, "Fred found a little bug on the playroom carpet, toddled over to the bug, sat down next to it and said, 'Hi Mr. Bug. I'm Fred.' Then he ran over to the chalkboard, picked up a green chalk, drew a bunch of circles, lines and squiggles and said, 'Mr. Bug, I make you a spider web to play.'"

My daughter ended the text with, "His mind!"

I wrote back, "I think it's his *heart* (not only his mind) that melts me. He has inborn empathy, and he teaches us these deep levels of kindness; to bugs, to trucks."

After reading the texts, my son called in tears and said,

"Mom, how many people would have squashed that bug? Ma, it's like me at my arts high school. All of us students there were like those bugs who so many teachers before had tried to squash. Then we went to this creative, empathic school where the teachers opened up—for us artistic types— safe webs, safe places for us to play."

Fred has taught us to stop, to listen, to hear others, even trucks, even bugs.

The next week we video chatted. Fred told me he had seen a big fish at the Aquarium tank. He said, "Susu, I scared. But I walk to glass and I touch it and I all done scared."

When I was young, I thought, and sometimes still do, that I'd have to have courage or take yet another communication course to be all-done-scared. Only if I were all-done-scared could I put out my hand, lean beyond my comfort zone, reach out. I believed I could only do something like Fred approaching the bug or the fish tank after I was all-done-scared, that my openess could only be in the future.

But Fred teaches how to walk up to fear—like meeting that bug or staring at the fish——and not only say "Hi," or squash or judge, but to say, "Hello, fear." From my three-year-old teacher, I'm learning to start right now to make friends with the bugs in my life, and to make webs for us to play together.

To Persist in Being Heard

Bob & Fred 9 • Laudie 7 • Cookie 4

"I want Mommy. I miss Mommy," Cookie wailed in her bedroom in Massachusetts while her mom was on a flight home from a work assignment.

My four grandchildren had read books, attempted Hoverboard skills, opened and closed a pretend shoe store, hugged, sprinkled a self-made creative mix of cinnamon and powdered sugar on toasted bagels. Cookie had laughed, joked, run around and talked, talked, talked. Now, after a bath with bath balm that turned the water fairy-dust pink, it was bedtime. She started to cry.

"I miss Mommy. I want Mommy."

I floated out ways to take her out of her misery.

"I miss mommy too."

Not a match for her feelings, my words were a clumsy empathic miss. She repeated her lament, at greater volume, as if to say, "You don't get it."

"I miss Mommy. I want Mommy."

In my next attempt, I held her, cradled her, enveloped her as her mom does. "I bet Mommy misses you too. I bet right now she is on the plane thinking, 'I miss Cookie.'"

She flailed her fist and increased the pitch, "I want Mommy."

Oops. Goofed again.

I hugged her and pulled the covers over both of us. "The sooner you go to sleep, the sooner you'll see mommy because she's coming home at midnight and she'll be here when you wake up."

She yanked the blanket to her side. "No! I need to stay awake so I can see her *the second* she walks in that door."

I thought doing some math might help her mind distract itself. "It's eight o'clock now. Mommy will be home at twelve midnight. How many hours is that?"

Seven-year-old Laudie, in the bed on the other side of the room, said, "Four."

Cookie, wiping tears from eyes squinted, pouted, "Four hours is a long time."

I said, "That's why it would be good for you to fall asleep soon and when you wake up," I poofed my hands open, "you'll see her."

"But I want Mommy to cuddle me before I go to sleep."

I said, "Yes, of course. She will."

As if to correct me, she added, "But I want her *now*."

I had thrown nothing but curveballs, so I tried a new pitch, one that intended to investigate, to get curious, rather than to correct her thinking, or erase her feelings. "How much do you miss her?"

I separated my thumb and forefinger about two inches apart. "This much?" Then I widened my open-palmed hands about two feet apart, "or this much?"

Cookie splayed herself on the fuzzy comforter and stretched her arms snow angel big. "I miss Mommy *this* much."

I said, "Wow! That's a lot!"

She flashed me her full-of-wonder, wonder-full eyes and said, pushing the stretch further, "Yup, even more."

I spread-eagled my arms, "And I bet she misses you *this* much."

Finally heard, she huddled with her four or five lovies and yawned, "I'm tired."

To Be A Cheerleader

Bob 4

Bob smiled, jumped and said, "Susu, can you do this?"

I said, "I don't know. I'll try."

Like an Olympic gymnast, Bob hopped onto the back of the playroom sofa with its soft upholstery over a solid wooden frame. He swung his legs and crawled his arms as if on a balance beam.

He landed his dismount and said, "See, like that. It's easy. Watch again."

I watched. Bob scooted his way from one end to the other a few times, a gleeful easy back and forth. No effort, just a joyous glide, legs smooth and rhythmic, feet hallway up the sofa back, knees straight, face simultaneously serious at this task and lit with delight.

I said, "Well, I used to be able to do this. Let's see if my shoulders are strong enough now."

Bob's blue eyes widened. He nodded *yes*. "You can do it.

All you have to do is try."

I tried. My arms buckled. I could not get my legs off the ground. My body tightened. His body relaxed as he floated through the air. A trainer would say his strength-to-weight ratio compared to mine favored him for this trick. My elbows gave way. My feet hit the floor rather than slide across it like Bob's repetitive and happy arc on the back of the sofa.

The young optimist encouraged, "That's okay. Try again."

I tried again. This time I held myself in position after the first leap onto the sofa. I wobbled.

Bob clapped, "That's great. Now go across."

As soon as I lifted one arm, the other collapsed. I fell again. My daughter entered the playroom and Bob said, "Mommy, Mommy, watch Susu."

I hoisted myself into another clumsy attempt. She said, "Mother, your shoulder. Your back. Please stop."

Undaunted, Bob turned from his mom to me, "Susu, you just have to practice. That's what I did. I couldn't do it at first. Then I kept trying. Look. Watch. Now I can."

I looked, "I see. Bob, how about if Susu stops now? I'll practice when I go back to Maine and we'll see how I do next time I come back, okay?"

He said, "Sure, but you have to practice."

I practiced. Still, I could not make the correct moves with my arms and legs. But going across didn't matter to me anymore. My days of high school gymnastics ended long ago. The joy of Bob's positivity and enthusiasm never ended. Every time I jumped onto the back of the sofa, I laughed as if Bob—my joy teacher—was with me smiling. Just as he taught me, I'd say, "That's okay, Susu." And I'd clap for myself.

To Be A Coach

Bob & Fred 6

My daughter and her friends with their children were on vacation in Florida with our family and other families. Fully six-years-old, full of fun, adventure and risk, Bob had played all week with these friends, his brother, and siblings.

One day, I joined them in the warm, sparkly blue pool, big enough for rowdy kids and the quieter adults who watched them. Bob invented rules to a game we played. I was to stay in one spot in the water. My feet could touch the bottom. The water covered most of my body. I threw a football as high as I could. Each in turn, one child jumped from the edge of the pool (probably a lifeguard's forbidden move). He or she caught the ball midair and then plopped into to pool.

They instructed me. "Susu, up higher, can you throw it up higher?"

I said, "I'm not sure. I'll try."

Bob said, "It's okay. Susu, just do the best you can."

Then someone, maybe a six-year-old girl or maybe a four-year-old boy, said, "How about you throw it sideways this time?"

Bob okayed that, "Susu, you can do that. Sideways would be fun for you."

Fred hollered, "Throw it long and far, not so high."

Bob said, "Susu, maybe you can try that too. If it works for you, you can go for it."

I tried. But my 68-year-old right shoulder pinched. My aim was no longer what it was when I was a catcher on my high school softball team.

I threw an off-kilter pass. Bob leapt with his someday-I'll-be-a basketball-player jump and, of course, missed the catch as it had spiked from my shallow end to somewhere in the middle of the deep end.

I said, "Oh, Bob, oops. Sorry." We laughed together. "I am so sorry, Bob. Yikes. My throw is waaaay waaaay off."

He said, "No, no, Susu, it was my fault. I jumped too soon. Just keep trying. Let's try again."

He changed the drill, "Maybe try to throw it this way."

He demonstrated a Tom Brady throw. I performed my grandmotherly throw. He missed it, of course, not possible to catch a ball three feet away.

He said, "Susu, I am so sorry. My fault on that one. I didn't have my eye on the ball."

Then he announced to the others, "Okay, wherever Susu throws it, that's where we catch it."

Bob created new rules for my old arm. Soon the young ones chanted, "Okay, Susu, just do the best you can. This is fun. I'm glad you are playing with us."

Bob coached kindness. The others followed.

To Share

Bob 7

My husband and I had designed it that way, a kitchen big enough for both of us to putter, to cook, or more truthfully spacious enough for us to prep our simple meals: steam colorful veggies, cut carrots, cucumbers, celery, romaine for a salad, figure out the rest from what's in the fridge or cupboards.

Early one morning when the grandkids visited, we thought we'd get a head start on breakfast. My husband was at the gas burners next to the smooth, gray counter. He faced the wall, the stove, the oven. He stirred eggs—whoosh, whoosh, whoosh—in his scratched non-stick pan. He then sidestepped to the other end of that counter to toast bagels. The room smelled of onion, slightly over-toasted. Bob dashed into the kitchen.

He saw Papa at the deep, wide farm sink. Bob watched his grandfather rinse the yellow ceramic bowl that had scrambled the yellow eggs.

I stood at the longer counter on the island, my back to my husband's. I faced the open living room with its early morning light brightening the soft gold on the walls. I rinsed blueberries and strawberries in the tiny sink at the edge of that island.

Bob looked at his papa and me, together yet separate at our tasks. He glanced from him to me and back again. He paused as if trying to figure something out, and then asked two questions.

"Why do you have two sinks in your kitchen?"

I said, "Well, sometimes, Papa and I are both cooking together at the same time and we wanted to have two sinks since that might be easier."

Then Bob posed an important life inquiry, "Can't you just share?"

To Be Nice

Bob & Fred 4

On a family ride one day, scrunched between Bob and Fred's car seats, I silently scanned the text message copied to me from our thirty-one-year-old son who had written his fourteen-year-old friend, Sam. He had reported to our son that he wanted to quit school—because of bullying, the not-so-secret notes passed about him, the slaps. Our son told Sam about his own life at fourteen: the tormenting in the school halls, harassment on the soccer field, the name-calling, being thrown against lockers. I cried.

Our son had responded to Sam, "You'll survive despite your childhood friends turning on you. You'll even thrive if you use this middle school horror as a way to stay steady, to get stronger. Sam, you're the most mature and resilient fourteen-year-old I know. You're going to be fine. More than fine."

Tears drenched my glasses. When my grandsons saw me, Bob asked, "what's wrong, Susu?"

I said, "I'm reading something and I feel sad about it."

Fred asked, "Why are you sad?"

I said, "Because I'm reading about how some people were not nice to other people."

Bob asked, "Were they mean?"

I sighed, "Yes."

Together Bob and Fred chorused, "Why can't those people be nice? Why would anyone be mean?"

Had these four-year-olds already chosen the value of kindness? Will their belief in goodness last? *Right then I remembered my Dad. I wished he had heard their sweet innocence. He would have agreed. Once I wanted to lash back at that popular girl Nikki Wasinki who told me, "You are not good enough for our group."*

Dad said, "You gotta go to bed with yourself at night. You gotta sleep with what you did all day. Don't be mean."

I act mean sometimes when later I wished I'd smiled. I am still trying to be nice when it's hard. I still miss my Dad because I think he would tell me, as our son did Sam, to get up every day and do my best, to put my head on my pillow at night feeling okay about how I'd acted. And now the wise, gentle and enormously innocent barely-out-of-toddlerhood children have channeled their great-grandfather and their uncle. They, too, teach the simplicity of "Why can't people be nice? Why would anyone be mean?"

Patience

All shall be well. And all shall be well.
And all manner of things shall be well.
—*Dame Julian of Norwich*

To Take Nothing Personally

Bob 4 · Laudie 2

"Mommy, Mommy," Laudie woke up from her nap and called out for her mom who was visiting newborn Cookie at Beth Israel Hospital. "Mommy, mommy, get me out of my cwib."

I slipped open her door, tiptoed into her room and sunny-dispositioned my greeting, "Hi Laudie! You're awake!"

Laudie stared at me through her tousled blonde curls and screamed, "I want Mommy."

I said, "Ya, me too."

"I want Mommy, too." If she only knew how much I meant this. "She'll be home soon. Do you want me to get you out of your crib?"

Laudie sobbed, hid her head under her lovey and kicked her feet, "*No! I don't want you. I want mommy to get me out.*"

As if a toddler-whisperer, I put my finger to my lips and murmured, still cheery-like smiling, "Awwwww, Sweetie, I

90

wish Mommy were here too. I can lift you out if you want."

She wailed and pounded her crib, "Susu, No! I don't want you!"

I said, "Okay. I'll leave your door open. Bob and I will play in the hall on the carpet where you can see and hear us. If you decide you want to play with us, you can let me know. I'll pick you up right away."

Thought monsters invaded my brain. "After all I've done for her...Blah, blah, blah. I hope she likes me... What if she doesn't? Maybe I don't like her so much right now either. So there!"

She trantrumed in her crib for twenty minutes, watching us build with Magnatiles and then announced, "Susu, I'm ready to get out now."

Later that week, Laudie bounced into my guest bedroom at six o'clock, huge tears wetting her cheeks. She wiped her eyes. I could not hear her words through her sobs. I said, "Laudie, you're crying. I can't understand what you are saying."

She wrapped her tiny arms around my broad shoulders, snuggled her wet face into my neck as she choked out, "Susu, Mommy just told me you are leaving today. I am so sad. I don't want you to leave. Please don't leave. I don't want you to go."

To Take Deep Bweffs

Bob & Fred 5 · Laudie 3 · Cookie 1

On her drive to Maine—minivan loaded with a week-end full of strollers, backpacks, Desitin, fleeces, pac-and-plays and Fred, Bob, Laudie and Cookie—my daughter called me to make plans. I could hear three-year-old Laudie strapped into her car seat in the second row behind her mother.

Laudie yelped in that bothering and interrupting way kids do when they know a parent directs attention away from them, "Mommy, Mommy."

Laudie loves to chat, loves to sing, and often babbles through the whole two-hour ride to Maine. It is often sweet, endearing. This was different. Bold. Intrusive. Strident.

My daughter turned up the phone's volume to hear me, yet couldn't. She said, "Wait a minute, Mom."

She addressed Laudie, "I'm talking to Susu. I'll be right with you, Laudie."

Laudie screamed, "Mommy, Mommy."

My daugther said, "Mom, I'll call you back."

When she called, all screaming had stopped. She planned, "We'll go swimming on Friday, and try to see friends on Sunday. I'll leave Cookie with you for a bit while I go for a run and.... and.... and..."

When I saw the black van pull into my driveway, I scooted out the door to hug everyone. My daughter winked at me and asked Laudie, "Laudie, do you have something to say to Susu?"

Laudie widened her huge blue eyes, froze in place, avoided my gaze and said nothing. Her mom knelt and rested her hands on Laudie's shoulders, "Laudie, you can do this."

Laudie's posture straightened, "Susu, I weawwy sowwy I wouldn't let you talk to Mommy."

I crouched on the blacktop next to her, wrapped my arms around her, pursed my lips to hide a smile.

Her mom whispered to Laudie, "What else?"

Laudie shook her head, stalled. Her mom offered, "Laudie, do you want me to help you?"

Laudie took a big breath, made eye contact with me, stood tall and said, "I won't do it again."

I kissed her forehead and nodded, "Mmmm."

Her mother continued, "What else?"

Laudie shrugged. Her mom coached, "If you feel disappointed, what are you going to do? If you feel impatient, what will you do next time?"

Laudie beamed, now grounded in her stance and gave her solid answer, "Take weawwy deep bweffs."

She embraced me; I her. I said, "Wow, what a great idea. I like to take deep breaths too when I don't get what I want, when I feel mad or sad. But sometimes I forget. You've reminded me to breathe. Thank you. You taught me."

Spiritual traditions teach that deep healing comes from the breath. Taoism says breathing is a way to purify. When "God breathed into him the breath of life," Adam became a living soul; hence Christians, Jews and Muslims know that breath is life. Buddhists teach that breathing awareness is a way to nurture mindfulness. Hindus say there is a correlation between our breathing and our thinking.

From small beautiful Laudie came a small beautiful practice; take deep breaths. What will I do next time I feel disappointed or impatient? Breathe.

To Stay in the Game
to Get to Yes/Yes

Bob & Fred 4 • Laudie 2

The red, foam toy truck I brought Fred to hold during medical tests was tiny. It was old. It was junk. Fred decided it was his favorite.

He arrived home from the hospital a few hours later carrying a goody bag filled with a miniature Lego set, a toy airplane with a plastic fuselage and cardboard wings, and his now-preferred truck.

His twin brother Bob rifled through the bag, grabbed the truck and vroomed it on his hands and knees dashing around the kitchen and living room floor. Fred seized it and screamed, *"No! It's mine!"*

Bob shouted, "No! We have to share."

They tussled. Fred yelled, "Susu gave that to me to go to the hospital."

Fred darted to his mom, who was cutting watermelon in the kitchen. He cried, "Bob took my truck and it's *no fair*."

Bob yelled from the living room, "I got it first just now and it's *no fair* for him to have it. We have to share."

Their mom, a teacher of social-emotional learning and ways to empower kids to make decisions, said, "Fred, you know how to solve a problem. You can go back and figure it out with your brother."

I saw this as a perfect opportunity for an intervention I had taught them that Fred had once dubbed "a brilliant idea." This method creates a pause, to teach them to be re-sponse-able—able to respond—instead of react. To have more choices than to snatch and squabble.

I plunked down between them and rolled open my palm, "Hand over the truck."

I turned my closed fist toward my belly to hide the prize, "Okay, we need to do that S.TO.P. thing that always works. Let's see if we can get to 'yes, yes.' Remember? Everything's workable. You can do this."

Their two-year-old sister Laudie, unable to pronounce "r", and with her usual silliness, added, "yes, it's weawy woke-able."

I laughed, "Okay. Let's start by stopping."

The first step in the acronym STOP: S for Stop.

They settled, Fred sitting to my right, Bob standing to my left.

I cheered, "Yay! Good stopping. Now we take a breath." (T in the acronym).

We inhaled, paused and exhaled, paused. I said, "Now let's take a look at what's going on." (O for observe)

The boys debated: "It's not fair."

"He shouldn't…."

"We need to…"

"Mommy and Daddy say…"

"It's mine…"

I shushed, "Shhh. Okay. You both want different things. Bob wants to play with the truck and Fred doesn't want to share. What are we going to do? Let's see if we can make a Plan (P) you can both say *yes* to."

Bob offered, "We can time it. I can have it for one minute and then Fred can have it for one minute."

Fred claimed, "No! That's not a plan! It's mine. Susu brought it for me!"

I said, "That's true. I had only one of those and I gave it to Fred for his doctor's visit."

I Stopped, Took a deep breath or two, then Observed. What do I prefer? That they have one more lesson in sharing? That one of them wins? I trusted this process more than I cared about the outcome, so we Proceeded (another P). What I secretly wanted was to hurry up, to end it, to decide for them.

After taking another breath, Fred posed, "Bob, you know how you have that favorite truck? And you know how you never want to share it?"

Freezing his eyes and face, yet willing to stay in this process, Bob mumbled "uh-huh."

Fred continued, "Well, that's how I feel now. I love this truck and I do *not* want to share it."

I exclaimed, "Whoa. This is new information. Is that true, Bob? Do you have a favorite truck that you don't like to share?"

I had no idea where this would lead, now that they owned the process, now that they had stopped pushing and pulling.

"Remember, everything is workable," I reminded.

"How about this? We play with each other's trucks. I play with his. He plays with mine. Yes, yes," said Fred and he nodded.

I said, "Okay. One yes. We have to get to both of you saying yes."

Bob stomped his feet, "No. I don't want anyone playing with my truck."

I stalled, "Ohhhhh. Hmm."

Fred agreed to the compromise, "Bob, that would be fair."

Bob sat, still now, rolled his eyes, pursed his lips and inhaled, "Fred, you can have the foam truck."

I asked, "So you both say 'yes' to that? You're both okay with Fred having the foam truck?"

They said, "Yup."

I said, "So we Stopped, we Took a breath, we looked at what was going on (Observed), we made a Plan and we got to 'yes, yes.' It's because you stuck with it a long time."

We high-fived. Bob smiled and said, "We did it. We stayed in the game until we got an answer. That was hard. But it was a good work-out."

Presence

You have to pick the places you don't walk away from.
—Joan Didion

To Be Here Now

Bob & Fred 11 months

Eleven-month-olds know how to gather crumbs. Bob stopped mid-crawl to inspect the only dust bunny in the corner. He turned its gray strands over in his tiny palm, began the lift to his mouth before I swapped a yellow measuring cup for the dust bunny. He laughed and flipped the newly received plastic back and forth, banged it upside down and right side up.

After playtime, Bob explored his highchair tray dotted with finger-food Puffs, toddler snacks not unlike the Cheerios I used to give his mother at the same age. He plunked his first finger into a Puff and raised it to his lips.

If he missed, he bunched up its pieces from his sticky cheeks, smooshed them onto his wet chin and clapped when they landed on his tongue.

What if we, too, woke up to the Cheerio-size marvels in life?

Fred took minutes to run his pointer finger along the spotted pattern in the carpet; open hand, open mind. He then folded his hands in prayer position in front of his sweet face and scanned the specks on his fingers.

What if we, too, cherished such miracles?

Eleven-month-olds could teach us a thing or two about joy. I watched Bob and Fred with their singular attention to what was right in front of them. I missed the delight of that attention when my mind flashed to grown-up concerns. *Should I buy scallions at Whole Foods or the Farmer's Market tomorrow? What if it pours for Becca's beach wedding next weekend? Do I have the right clothes for my Virginia trip next month?*

My mind busy with scattered themes and schemes, I spotted Bob as he scurried to me with a tiny plastic electrical outlet cover in his mouth, the little protectors to keep children's mouths from shocking currents. My daughter assured me her son had not pulled this out of a socket; he found it on the floor, one of those crumbs he couldn't overlook, one of those everyday surprises in his path that calls for time, interest and inquiry.

After I traded Bob his much-loved orange teething ring for the outlet cover, he smiled and waddled off, as Fred toddled to me to research the shiny buttons at the loose collar of my shirt. Touch. Look. Taste. My thoughts, though, wandered to the tightly buttoned shirt of spiritual teacher Eckhart Tolle on TV.

Fred stayed at my neck. I, on the other hand, traveled on a mind romp. I wondered, *Would Eckhart's buttons shine? His work surely shines, like his book,* The Power of Now. *Will I ever finish reading that? His writing and his humor sparkle. I like him. I don't understand him fully. I hope he keeps giving talks. Maybe I can find him on YouTube. I'll check Amazon, too.*

My adult brain had flown to the future while Tolle's simple be-here-now message and the wide-eyed twins aimed to teach presence.

Maybe to be happy, we need to take care of the crumbs, to regain our instincts toward joy. Perhaps childlike attention could lead us. If we gather crumbs—waves from neighbors, rainbows—maybe we'd unhide the hidden beauty around us. If we learned from eleven-month-olds, we might think less and feel more. We might discover their secrets for laughing and giggling and their ever-unfolding sense of awe.

To Find and Own Our Voice

I remember Laudie's birth. My husband and I paced in the Virginia hospital, waiting for the scheduled c-section. We ate flaky pastries. We made small talk with others, "Are you new grandparents?" "Where are you from?" "Is your daughter or daughter-in-law having a baby?"

I remember the delivery nurse's news, "All are fine. The baby looks great. Mom is doing well."

I remember seeing our third grandchild for the first time, wrapped in a pink and white striped soft blanket, having her mom introduce us to her, hearing her name for the first time, which had been chosen a while ago. I remember we cried.

I remember I wore that teal blouse. I wore that teal shirt for its color, its floral design, the feel of lightness in the jersey fabric. I wanted comfort that day.

I remember that Laudie's two-year-old, twin brothers called her their "new baby sister."

I remember Laudie cried. She cried a lot. Even after a few days of life, I remember we said things like, "Wow, she sure has a mind of her own." or "Well, this little girl will let us know what she wants." or, "You got a strong one."

I remember babysitting for Laudie once in Maine. Her two-year-old twin brothers finally sound asleep, I was exhausted. At midnight, my husband woke me up to tell me Laudie was screaming. He had not been able to calm her. He had tried what he knew; rocking, shushing. "Maybe she needs a bottle?" he asked.

Half-asleep and in a fog, I sat on the stairs to hold her and sing to her. I was afraid of dropping her. I could not move my muscles. So, we sat, me with my fear, she with her scream.

I remember years later Laudie tantruming in her crib for half an hour refusing to let me pick her up and out. Screaming "I want Mommy." Did I mention, this girl has a mind of her own?

I remember one Halloween, when the twins were five and Laudie three, how Fred masterminded a brilliant plan for their costumes. He would be a lobster, but so big that—in the story he created—he would have to be thrown back into the ocean. Cookie, at seven months, would also be a lobster, but so small, she, too, would belong to the ocean. Bob would be a lobster boat. Laudie would be a lobster trap. Baby Cookie happily let her mom dress her as a lobster. Bob helped in the design and painting of his boat, carving his huge costume out of a box, pasting it with lobster stickers. Fred proudly ran around the neighborhood in his red lobster suit. Laudie said, "I do not want to be a lobster trap. I am going to be a piggy."

My daughter has said girls need to find their voice. I think we found our teacher.

To Learn Sports

Bob & Fred 7 · Laudie 4 · Cookie 2

Super Bowl 2018. Patriots vs. Eagles. The four grandchildren took a nap or at least attempted a quiet time that Sunday afternoon, part of the deal if they wanted to watch the game. We had prepared snacks. In their elementary school in Massachusetts, only three out of 253 students would root for the Eagles. Two-year-old Cookie, who didn't yet go to school, held up three fingers and said, "Only fwee."

Bob and Fred had been granted special privileges. Usually in bed by seven, tonight they could cheer on their team. They had eaten pizza at five o'clock, had early baths, pulled on their cotton pajamas, and thrilled to be sitting on the sofa with their younger sisters and me. We held navy blue, plastic cups Patriots' Logo-ed in one hand and, in the other, cheddar goldfish crackers. They wore plastic bracelets, each in their favorite color, with printed words like "Go Pats" or "Game On." We were ready.

The game began.

The boys cheered, "So great that Gronk is out of concussion protocol. Yay! He can play."

News to me.

Laudie asked, "How do you say that Danny guy's last name? Aaaaaamendola or A*men*dola?"

Bob said, "Wait and see what the broadcaster says."

I wondered, who is Amendola?

Laudie asked, "Susu, want me to tell you what I know about football."

"Sure. What?"

"Tom Brady is not always on the field."

I bet she knew more about football than I did.

Cookie dragged her blankies, loveys and dolls (her "babies") from her crib to her staked-out corner of the comfy sofa. "I wuv the Supabow!"

Ten minutes after the first kickoff she said, "My babies need bottles, my blankies don't cover my feetsies," and while watching tackles and catches, "when does the Supabow start?"

Cookie slept as soon as she tucked in her babies. Laudie yawned and rubbed her eyes for the first half and through Justin Timberlake's half time music, then dozed into five or six of her rainbow-colored pillows.

The boys followed every play. "Brady will hand off this time. I know he will."

How did they know this?

And, "Wow, a first down. The Eagles are playing well, Susu."

I wondered who got that first down.

They admitted, "It's a good game."

Yet every time the Eagles scored, one of them jumped off the sofa, "Ugh! Patriots' defense is bad!" Or, "The Patriots are not playing well."

I said, "Sure they are. They're in the Super Bowl. The Eagles are just playing great."

They paid no attention. At the last few seconds of the fourth quarter, three and a half hours after their normal bedtime, my granddaughters slept; the boys perched on the edge of their cushions. Pats were down. Their only hope was a miracle. Brady had the ball deep in the Eagles territory (I'd learned some of their lingo, didn't know what it meant). Bob crossed his fingers, "Tom needs to throw a bomber."

I asked, "What's a bomber?"

Bob answered, "It means he has to throw it to the other end of the field."

At ten, maybe ten-thirty, these first graders slogged upstairs, dejected at the loss, elated to have witnessed the game. I had learned a few things from these true sports fans. Now I too wuv the Supabow.

To Be Assertive

Cookie 3

Cookie and I walked hand-in-hand into her pale blue bedroom with soft blue windowshades and pink pillows in her crib. She cradled her comfy loveys and the cloth dolls she called her babies. We stepped into her closet, dresses arranged with dresses, sweaters with sweaters, tights folded in neat piles. She pointed to a dress, solid navy blue on top, with a blue and white striped skirt. She said, raising her eyebrows, "That."

I said, "Okay."

She stood on tiptoes, reached, then sighed, "I can't weach it."

I pulled it off its hanger, careful not to mess up the neat arrangement, handed it to her and she slipped it on.

I said, "It's time for Papa and Susu to go back to Maine."

We headed to the door of the house, passing her three older siblings playing Fish before leaving for school. "Do you have any tens?"

"No, go fish."

"Come on! I just went fishing last time."

"You're peeking. No fair! That's cheating."

Their dad said, "Okay, kids. On the count of five. In the car with Mom. I'm off to work. Give Susu, Papa and me hugs."

Cookie and I stepped over Bob's Nike soccer cleats. We brushed aside Cookie's teeny carriage for her babies. We nearly crushed Fred's fishing pier he'd made from wooden blocks. We entered the garage, a storage room for bikes, some big hanging from giant hooks on walls, some small, surely outgrown, leaning in corners, in each child's favorite color. Orange. Green. Purple. Pink. I lugged my suitcase and my husband's canvas duffle bag, hard to maneuver around the kiddie kayak. I foot-planted gingerly so as not to crush Fred's dead frog on the floor, careful in the midst of this family's stuff. More familiar with the ground-plan, Cookie charged through and headed for my Subaru Outback parked in the street.

As we skipped on the wide blacktop driveway, Cookie spotted their black Honda and said, "Daddy took Mommy's car. I'm going in yours."

Her mom joined us and said, "Cookie, you can stay here with me."

I looked down at Cookie. Then I looked up at my daughter. Cookie looked around at both of us. Feeling the determination in this wide-eyed granddaughter, seeing the magical wonder of childhood creativity, and with a sense what bright, funny, new and difficult conversation might ensue, I lifted my gaze to the neighborhood to buy myself some time before saying whatever I might say next. It would take tact and kindness. I knew from experience: Cookie tantrums against power struggles. I saw maple trees with hints of autumn oranges on the tips of leaves. I saw the neighbor's house with seven construction vehicles in the driveway even after months of rehabbing a kitchen. I saw the cocoa-colored poodle next door asleep on his sidewalk.

I took a deep breath and turned to Cookie. "I soooo want you to come to Maine. Can't be today though. When would you want to come?"

"Now!"

I paused, "Hmmm. When you come maybe in a few weeks, what will you bring?"

She stomped her feet and pouted, "Right now, I'm bwinging my babies, five of them, and their bottles and their cwibs. Do you have woom for their cwibs? Oh, and my diapers. You have food, wight?"

I knelt and whispered, "Yes, Cookie, I'll have what you'll need. Today you get to stay with your family. Susu and Papa have to go home to work. Someday we'll plan it. Someday soon you'll come to Maine. Yes, I have room for your five babies and their cribs and I have food."

She folded her arms across her chest, "I want to come today. Can you go get my booster seat? You need a booster seat for me."

To Read, Really Read

Cookie 4

She tsk-tsked, "These kinds of books are for babies."

Cookie frowned when I showed her a tiny board book at bedtime one night as my choice for a goodnight story. She repeated, "And I mean babies."

I said, "Oh? I didn't know. I like the pictures. Can we enjoy the artwork?"

"No," she plopped down and began to teach me how to choose books.

She picked a 10-inch by 10-inch colorful book from her overflowing bookshelf near the door of her pink bedroom. *Ahh, picture books must be appropriate for her age*, I thought.

She jumped with it onto her bed and we snuggled together on top of her fuzzy furry comforter.

"Not under it," she said, "that's for later when I go to sleep."

Then I knew three things:

1. Board books are for babies.
2. Picture books are for pre-school kids.
3. Nighttime reading happens on top of the sheets and blankets.

We studied the smiling boy on the cover of *If I Built a House* by Maine author Chris Van Dusen. I knew this delightful book, filled with a young boy's imagination of a dream house he would design. I'd read it many giggly times to her two older twin brothers (when they were in pre-school of course). I looked forward to having Cookie hear it too.

I said, "Look at this. So colorful. See the face of the boy's dog? What do you think that dog is imagining?"

She fingered the corners and edges of the page, "Susu. Open the book. Turn the page."

Lesson: 4. Read at the pace of the child.

I opened to the inside cover page and pointed out, "See this? A funky chimney."

She said, "Susu, this is not the book. Turn the page."

Lesson: 5. Turn pages at the rate of the child.

We began. I knew enough to skip the title page—not interesting to a four-year-old for sure—fascinating as the main character was to me, sitting at a picnic table with tools, pencils, Legos, tinker toys, and scotch tape.

At the start, I read the way adults read. I spoke the letters and words, finished the rhyme, turned the page, and rolled onto the next stanza. I assumed Cookie would listen. We learned about Jack and his boundless enthusiasm for invention. But by the time we landed at his All-in-one Kitchen-o-Mat and I was ready to move to his living room trampoline and giant ball pit, Cookie halted my hand from flipping the page.

"Look. They have pizza," Cookie said.

I rushed, "Uh-huh and on the next page there's a cool room."

She flattened the pizza page and pointed to a painting of a bowl filled with what looked like tan dough with little brown dots and hands on the end of tubes mixing it. Her eyes lit up as she asked, "Wait! Do you think it's chocolate chip cookies?"

I checked my watch. Countdown to bedtime. *My*

goal? Dash to the finish.

I pushed, "I don't know. Let's turn the page."

Cookie's goal was to dig into what was right there. "No, not yet. Look here. Jack's having a cheeseburger and French fries for dinner. Do you like hamburgers and French fries?"

Hurried, I tried a short answer, "No."

"Okay. Well, I like them," she said as she turned the page.

My mind raced. My stomach clutched. I had lost the magic in the miraculous power of reading aloud to kids, the way kids want, the way kids love. I said, "Come on!"

We managed a few flowing pages. I thought, *What happened to cover-to-cover? The right way to read a book.*

But moving too fast out of a present moment experience was not Cookie's way, nor is it the only way, maybe not the right way, if there is a right way to read a book.

When we arrived at the page with the huge bedroom on top of a 200-foot tower, I pointed to the glass surrounding it. She pointed to a tiny drawing—a woman and a dog on the sidewalk looking up at the sky and this flying room, and asked, "Do you think this lady is the dog's owner?"

I remembered Lesson Four: Read at the pace of the listener, so I put my hands down and slowed with her, "Hmm…What do you think? She could be a dogwalker?"

Cookie said, "No, Susu, dog walkers don't get dressed up fancy like that."

"Well, maybe it's a grandmother visiting like I'm here with you."

She cuddled, cozied up, "Susu, do you think her dress is red or pink?"

Finally, in this enchanted time together, I said, "I don't know but I like those polka dots. Do you?"

And so it went. We read and stopped. We chatted and connected. Curious about the main character, his dog, his mother, together we asked, "Does the mom look happy in this picture?"

Cookie wasn't stalling to put off bedtime. She wasn't interrupting. She wasn't asking ridiculous questions. She was teaching patience, humility, and that books should be read with joy, laughter, enjoying what's on the page, at the pace of presence.

Stillness

*You must learn to be still in the midst of activity and
to be vibrantly alive in repose.*
—Indira Gandhi

To Sit, Just Sit

Bob & Fred 2

I'd wondered what I might call a bigger-than-me energy. God? Nature? The Universe? Mystery? Then my visiting grandsons handed me an epiphany in my living room. Wearing flip-flops as I cleaned, I'd wipe countertops, dust, and make beds while Bob and Fred played choo-choo-train with our now-grown son's wooden Brio set. Bob or Fred would say, "Susu, shoes off. Sit." They would squat, pat the floor next to them and gesture for me to stop the busyness and play with them, be with them. Simple.

The first time I heard, "Susu, sit," I smiled. Even though I drudged on with my grown-up chores, I grasped what the babies were telling me in their happy innocence: "We are here. Be with us. Let's enjoy each other. This time is precious."

The second time I heard, "Shoes off. Susu, sit," I stopped; rather I was stopped. I felt like a lightning rod electrified by a huge charge, perhaps like Moses must have felt when he heard, "Take off your sandals. You are standing on holy ground."

"Susu, sit" awakened me to the wonder in front of me, my own version of the burning bush. This waking up paled compared to Moses' but it felt huge. I got it: the boys, as guides, invited me into presence.

When I listened, or more exactly when I heard them, when I took off my shoes and sat with them, the true miracle came.

After I plunked myself down, they said, "Close."

They snuggled into me, wriggled right next to me, hip to hip. I felt them. I felt us. I knew this spot on the deep green basement carpet was indeed sacred ground.

Bob and Fred returned to their home, but the echoes of these young teachers resonated, rippled. In my forgetfulness, I felt abuzz in adult activity again, clomping around in my flip flops, picking up dropped sippy cups and pajamas left under the pac-and-play. I whizzed along at dizzying speeds. Sometimes I remembered, "Susu, sit." I knew I had heard important words, *Sit and move in close to simplicity and innocence*.

If we turn toward it, the message of the wise children, "Sit. Close," is not so far away. Maybe we just have to listen.

To Relax

Fred 2

Fred crept across the soft playroom carpet to pull a board book from the shelves, trotted back across the long room, landed in my arms, turned himself around, plopped himself down, tucked himself into my lap, and leaned his back against my torso. I heard him release a deep breath. Ahhhh. That was it. We sat together and turned pages. We pointed at pictures, laughed.

I want to sit more often like this, like Fred. I want to let go into the lap of the Earth, as he let go into mine, to feel held as he snuggled into my hold. I could see Buddha's image in how Fred and I sat connected to the Earth. Solid.

I have been practicing letting my weight down into the Earth, sink as if being held and rocked. My only job, as Fred demonstrated, is to release my muscles. Slow down. Ahhhh.

It's enough.

Quiet. Silence. Nothing to do but let go. Laugh a little.

Stop Adulting

The secret of genius is to carry
the spirit of a child into old age.
—Aldous Huxley

To Yield to Imagination

Laudie 7 • Cookie 4

It started as a matching game. Cookie wanted to wear "exactly these green flip flops. These!"

We rummaged through the cloth bucket where shoes lived in her garage. Our fingers landed on gray crocks, pink sneakers, purple sandals. No tiny green flip-flops. Seeing the mélange of various types, sizes and which-shoe-goes-to-which-kid, I said, "Why don't we lay them out on the floor and see if we can match them up?"

"Na, Susu, that would be no fun. Boring."

I wasn't thinking of fun. I was thinking of order. The pile of footwear seemed, well, messy to me.

I dumped the conglomeration. As shoes hit the floor, out came socks, errant golf balls and directions for a skateboard. It looked like a yard sale or maybe a going-out-of-business display from a sporting goods store. *She wants it to be fun*, I thought and said. "Hey, Cookie, how

126

about we match things up and start a shoe shop?"

She smiled and started sorting. We invited Laudie to play.

"No, thanks," Laudie whispered "pretend" to me, then said, "I want to rest by myself then I am going to pack for a two-day hiking trip."

Cookie pouted, "Laudie doesn't want to play with me."

I knew that Laudie's imagined hiking trip could help us with our own imagination. I wondered if I could enter the world of childhood play, if I could let Cookie's creativity lead and see if I could respond in improvisational theater-style to any of her brainchilds, accepting any idea she put forth.

"Cookie, how are we going to set up the shelves?"

She turned over an Amazon box, newly delivered, "here, like this," she said as she made up a shelf. She then set up a shoe show, a few pair of pastel crocks displayed on the top.

I could have pointed out that mommy needed whatever was in that Amazon box. I could have been grown up. But I remembered improv ingenuity. I took a breath and reminded myself, "go with it."

Handing her two pairs of mud-covered gray and black crocks, I said. "Here are more. Do you want to put these there too?"

Store manager now, she said, "Susu, no! We only have these colors. We only sell girls' shoes. Pink. Purple. Light blue. Not those colors."

As employee, I asked, "Why don't we sell boys' shoes? They wear them too."

Fully in shoe store mode now, she said, "Because boys don't come into a shoe shop."

"Do you think maybe girls would buy crocks for their brothers?" I wondered aloud.

She furrowed her brow as if I had asked a stupid question and said, "Naaaa. Girls don't do that."

Laudie entered with a baby buggy filled with jackets, pillows, knit hats, snack bars and asked, "Do you have boots? I need boots for mud in case it rains on my hike."

Cookie raised her eyebrows to me, "Our first customer."

She gestured to her sister, "Sure, we have boots right over here."

She skipped to the pastel boots perched on a picnic cooler.

Laudie asked, "Could I rent the boots for two days? For my hike? Then return them?"

Cookie frowned, "No. We don't rent."

I forgot about saying *yes* to whatever this young entrepreneur offered and suggested. "We could rent."

She asserted her leadership and her vision for our shop. "We don't rent."

Laudie asked, "Are you sure you don't rent boots?"

I turned to Laudie, "Wait. I'd like to have a private business meeting with my boss here."

I whispered to Cookie. "If we rent, we can make more money. They'll pay now, and when they come back, we'll give them part of their money back, but not all of it. It'll help us."

She marched out of the conference and announced, "Okay. We'll rent but only two days a week."

I sensed an opening but wanted to make sure she still felt in charge. I said, "Okay. Perfect! Today is Tuesday. Can Tuesday be one of our rent days?"

Laudie paid us with crumpled leaves for money. Cookie stowed them in a baseball cap, the cash drawer, and we closed the shop for the day.

To Solve Problems

Laudie 5

Laudie asked me to read the book, *Penguin Problems*, by Jory John and Lane Smith. In the book one penguin complains about everything. "It's way too early." "My beak is cold." "It snowed some more last night, and I don't even like the snow." "It's too bright out here." "The ocean smells too salty today." "Oh, great. An orca. Oh, great. A leopard seal. Oh, great. A shark. What is it with this place?"

On and on.

Then a wise old walrus has the penguin think about the people in the world who love him, how the sun shines so bright and the moon is so pretty. He says, "Yes, some things are challenging. We all have difficult moments. But hear me…. I am certain that when you think about it, you'll realize that you are exactly where you need to be. Please think about what I've said, Penguin."

The complaining penguin seems to understand. The words make sense. "Maybe things will work out, after all."

But they don't and on the last page, the young penguin complains again.

I found the book cute, fun and a bit of a downer, a lesson about how life is tough sometimes.

I asked Laudie, "How 'bout this book?"

She said, "I like it."

I asked, "Oh. What do you like about it?"

She said, "I love this book because the penguin has problems and figures out how to solve them, so that helps *me* sometimes when I have problems and the penguin helps me figure out how to solve them."

I didn't correct her that it was the walrus who was wise. The penguin, stuck, gripes again even after the walrus' suggestions.

I asked, "What kind of problems do you have that penguins helps you solve?"

Laudie said, "Sometimes I am going up the chairlift to ski and I'm cold and my nose is freezing and I think I don't want to ski, but then I get off the lift and start to ski down and I think it's not so cold anymore."

I thought, *Wow. How did she get that from this book?* I said, "Hmm."

Laudie continued, "Or sometimes I go to the beach and

the water is so cold but the sun comes out and it's fun to play in the sand."

I could have left it at that. She got it. She had learned what she needed to learn. But the habit of adulting refused to fade. From Buddhist texts I remembered, "Every conditioned aspect of life is impermanent."

I persisted, "Yes, things can change, huh?"

I could have, should have, let go. She had polished her problem-solving acumen. She said, "Ya," and waved her arm in front of my face as if to say "Enough. I'm done with that."

She then called to her mother, "Mom you promised to read until you couldn't read anymore."

Still carrying on, I said, "Like you can think about things differently, right?'

No doubt exhausted from my teacher-ing, she nodded to me and said to her mom, "There's one more I want. Come on, two more books."

To Negotiate

In his driveway in Massachusetts, Bob jumped up and down and exclaimed, "Susu, Susu, Susu, we had soooo much fun and guess what?"

I widened my eyes and mouth as wide as his and belted, "*What*?"

He gestured with wild hands, "At the lake house where we stayed last summer in New Hampshire there was a kayak for kids and we *loved* it and I learned how to paddle it and we want one."

I repeated, "You want one?"

He lowered his voice, "Ya, but Daddy said they cost money."

I turned to their Dad, who nodded, "Yup, they do. I asked the kids if they had money to buy it. They said, 'No' so we've been brainstorming ways they could get money."

I asked the boys, "So what have you thought of?"

Mind conniving, Fred blurted, "We could steal some money......Naaaa. Just joking. That wouldn't be kind."

Laudie and Bob laughed, "No, he's kidding. But, Susu we have some good ideas. We don't take what isn't ours. What a silly idea to steal money."

I wanted to hear their method of getting what they wanted. "So, tell me your good ideas."

Bob said, "We could have a sale-yard and sell some of our toys."

I agreed, "Uh-huh."

Fred offered, "We could walk around the neighborhood and pick up coins that are on the ground."

I concurred, "Mmm-hm."

Laudie pointed to the end of the driveway, "We could sell lemonade."

Bob hopped into my lap, flashed his huge blue eyes, batted his long eyelashes, cozied up and started to bargain, "Susu, we thought maybe you could give us some money for our kayak."

"Clever," I thought and conceded, "Well, I could give you money."

I sought a counter-offer, "But if I give you money to buy a kayak, then I would own part of it, right?"

"Right," they agreed.

I asked, "So, could I use it? Would you share it with me?"

Bob parleyed, "No, Susu it's just for kids."

I said, "Hmmmm. Well then, how could we work that out if I gave you some money?"

Bob thought a long time, then tapped my shoulder and said, "win." He pointed at himself, said, "Win. Get it, Susu, win/win?"

With expansive thinking and sweet eight-year-old diplomacy, he posed his closing offer, "Well, Susu, because it's you, we could leave the kayak at your house, in your garage in Maine!"

Trust

Act boldly and unseen forces will come to your aid.
—Dorothea Brande

To Keep It Simple

Cookie 3

Cookie and I had colored, licked and stuck stickers, fingered and eaten a snack of Cheerios, read to her babies as they held lovies, and felt our way through Cookie's well-loved, first book *Pat the Bunny*. Now we were writing words with double oo in the middle. School. Brook. Tools. Smooch.

She had chattered cheerfully non-stop for two hours, "Pool. Food. Loop."

"Susu, can you help me count my Monopoly money? I have lots of money."

"Susu, my babies need their nap now."

"Susu, do you want play a game?"

Beyond tired, withered, and hoping the game had something to do with Cookie taking a nap with her dolls, I took a deep energizing breath, not knowing how long this new game might go on, and agreed, "Sure, what game?"

She said, "It's called Talk."

She had not stopped chatting all morning, so I wondered what could be new in Talk.

I smiled, "How do we play Talk?"

With her three-year-old muscular strength, she dragged two white chairs, both taller than her head, away from the dining room table. She grunted as she pushed and pulled them trying to place them together.

She groaned, "Ugh, Susu, this is hard. They are heavy."

I asked, "Can I help?"

"Nope," she chirped as she set them exactly where she wanted them. She was precise, two chairs side-by-side. "The chairs have to go like this. Now, here's how you play Talk. We each sit in one of these chairs and we talk."

"That's the game?"

"Yip."

My imagination could not match hers. I had to ask, "Talk about what?"

She reminded me of classroom order, "You have to stay in your chair. It doesn't matter what we talk about. You can make it up. What do you have to say?"

Adults could learn a few things about simplicity.

To Take Turns

Bob & Fred 4

"My turn."

"No, my turn."

"No fair."

For Fred and Bob's fourth birthday, my husband and I gave them "big boy bikes," orange, with an L.L. Bean decal on the chain cover, silver crossbars, black protective foam wrap on the handlebars and training wheels. They jumped on the cushy seats as soon as my brother assembled them. The physical part of riding—refining pedal-pushing, balancing, steering—posed no problem in their learning to ride. The rules of the road? Not so much.

Bob launched ahead of Fred, advanced to our nearby roundabout, "I'm winning. I'm first."

I saw this as an opportunity to coach them in staying focused on their own ride, a metaphor for having the life you want, a larger teaching of don't let your head get mixed up with what the other guy is doing. I proposed this thesis: "Being first isn't better."

I checked off a mental box and fist pumped, "yeah, me" for this lesson in mindfulness: non-judging.

Bob said, "Ya, ya, Susu, but I want to be the leader."

I didn't hear this antithesis—since I clung to my own agenda. I offered a potential synthesis, "How about we have a leaderless ride? You each get to go slow or fast or stop to see the beautiful fall leaves. It's a circle; being first doesn't matter."

Fred said, "Ya, Susu, but that's not fair because Bob was the leader before."

I did not, could not, accept what they said. I countered, "You're making it about only two choices. Either he's ahead or you're ahead. Maybe two choices is no choice in a circle. Maybe two choices is only a fight. We need a third thing."

They banged their new bikes into each other. They bolted out in front as they circled 'round and 'round. They looked at me with raised eyebrows and eyes squinting that hinted, "What is she talking about?"

I'm pretty sure they didn't understand "take your own ride" either. Or braking distance, which I thought a brilliant way to avoid the crashes they giggled over. "Stay at least one bike's distance behind the rider ahead."

I showed them at a cul-de-sac how to ride equidistant

around the trees and rocks, so they could feel no-leader, no-follower, so that they could experience the third thing. I said, "'You lead' or 'I lead' doesn't matter."

Bob said, "Ya, Susu, but I like winning."

Humbled by a four-year-old, I submitted, "Oh, Yes. Of course. We all do, Bob."

They said, "Okay. She finally gets it. Let's take turns being first."

To Stay Committed to a Cause

Bob & Fred 4

We crouched at what they called the frog pond, a neglected former fountain in their backyard, a place to climb, to find rock ledges and offer rousing performances of pre-school songs and dance moves.

I squatted near a leaf-cluttered pool, near muddied water surrounded by smooth egg-shaped rocks, like the black basalt stones massage therapists use when they offer hot stone massage. We were using random yard debris to build a bridge for inchworms so they wouldn't touch the water. I asked, "Why can't they go through the water? Wouldn't that be quicker for them?"

Fred stopped his serious stick-gathering and rolled his eyes, "Susu, I know a lot about inchworms and do you want me to tell you something?"

"Sure."

"They die in water. We can't let them touch the water."

"Hmm. I didn't know that."

He stood, looked up at me, "Ya, if you want to know anything about inchworms, just ask me. I am the director of this inchworm project."

I marveled at his grown-up vocabulary, shocked to hear "director," and "inchworm project." I asked, "What does a director do?"

He walked around the job site, "A director tells other people what to do. If you have any questions about how to build, you can ask me."

I said, "Okay. Fred. I don't see any inchworms here."

Fred looked at me with the inner knowledge of a four-year-old, no doubt wondering how his grandmother got through life so far. "Susu, if there's no inchworm village, they won't be here. We have to build them a place to come first. Then you'll see them."

I asked, "Oh, it's like, 'if we build it, they will come?'"

He stated, "Yup. See, Susu? I told you. I know a lot about inchworms. And I'm a good builder of villages for them."

"I see that. Have you built others?"

Out of the corner of my eye, across their lawn from our frog pond, I spotted Bob and Laudie "mountain biking" on a tiny hill.

They stopped their pedaling to build a teepee-type structure, with a collection of toy trucks and shovels around it.

They dug a little, raced each other a lot. They yelled to ask permission of the director: "Fred, is this okay? Can we add more sticks here?"

He yelled back, "Sure. Just be careful of the mud because sometimes mud has water in it, and inchworms can't have any water."

They said, "Okay."

Bob and Laudie rushed off to get their scooters and bikes then bombed up and down Mountain Bike Hill. They played. I asked Fred if he wanted to take a break and join them. But Fred was not playing, and it didn't matter to him that there were no inchworms anywhere. He said, "No, thank you, Susu. I need to keep building because I love inchworms, and they need me."

To Accept the Things
We Cannot Change

Laudie 6

"Paying attention to the breath is boring," first-grader Laudie said after a session of yoga-for-kids at a retreat center in Western Massachusetts.

I said to my granddaughter, whom I had hoped would be a budding yogini, "Really? Inhaling and exhaling?"

"Want me to show you I know how to do it?" she bragged.

Heartened by her interest, "Sure. Of course."

Laudie pulled and pushed the breath. She sounded like a freight train, blowing out, puffing in, forcing. We laughed. I wondered if breath might not be the doorway for her to calm herself when stressed. Breath is the portal to changes in the nervous system. Long slow outbreaths to relax; inbreaths for energy. I had so wanted her to have these tools, an inner pharmacopeia. I also admit to, "This is my way, the right way."

In the car later, Laudie happily buckled her seatbelt in the back seat behind the passenger's side. Click. I felt my weight sink into my seat for our ride home. We reached the summit of the Berkshires in a whirling April blizzard. Ice. Snow. Sleet. Rain. Howling wind. Ahead of us, cars slipped off-road landing in the frozen off-road bushes and trees. Trucks teetered on the slippery shoulders. We smelled the heavy exhaust. Hail landed on the windshield, stuck to it and blinded my view. The wipers swish-swished without clearing the buildup. I heard freezing rain pinging on the roof and hood. I could not see the road, the edge of the road, or the way ahead, and only so far as the chugging truck in front of me, heavy, tire chains rattling. My seatbelt felt tighter.

My thumping heart raced; armpits dampened. I shifted my body ten times. And then, my exhale lengthened. I began to take long, slow inhales and long, slow exhales. Five, maybe more, deep breaths. The easing of my breath matched the fierceness of the squalls. I made my breath silent so Laudie would not sense my underlying panic. In. Out. Repeat. I deliberately let my shoulders drop away from my ears on the outbreath. I let the inbreath fill me enough to imagine the air moving into the space in the body, head, and heart that tears would otherwise have occupied.

More snow. More ice. More road blindness. More cars in the ditch. Maybe twenty miles of it. Concerned, with furrowed brow and shoulders at my ears, I heightened my pitch and hinted to Laudie. "You know that calming breath you learned?"

Uninterested, she mumbled, "Mmm hmm. Boring."

Thinking she could reset fear, quell anxiety, practice this oh-so useful skill, I suggested, "This would be a good time to use it."

Rejecting my brilliant wisdom, she shook her blonde ponytail *No* and said, "Why? I love snowstorms and anyway, I'm coloring."

To Dare to Test Limits

Bob & Fred 5 · Laudie 3

I walked to their backyard to find Fred, Bob, and Laudie perched on high shaky branches, each in their own tree. I told them, "Whoa! If Susu is beneath Bob's tree and at the same time Laudie starts to fall, I won't be able to help her."

Fierce, Laudie fired, "I won't need you."

I said, "If Fred starts to fall, and I'm under Bob's tree, I can't catch Fred."

Fred insisted, "Susu, I am going to climb as high as I can, and this will be dangerous and definitely against the rules, but we love to climb."

My heart jumped. How to be a grandparent here? A hardline "no," or wait to see what happens?

I said, "I hear you. I love to climb too, but rules are made for safety. I don't feel safe with this idea."

Laudie, who hadn't learned to pronounce l and r held firm, "Weww, we feew safe. We wuv to cwimb."

Again, I said, "I *do* hear you and I don't feel comfortable with this."

Bobbing his head and gesticulating his arms, Fred's push-back continued. He said, "Well, if you hear me, then I should be able to do it. If you hear me, that means you'll let me do what I say. I am going to tie a wire around my waist. My body says it's safe, so up we go."

The boys climbed higher, ski helmets buckled on their heads. Laudie stayed closer to the ground. I had trouble seeing Bob and Fred hidden at the tops of the trees. How did I lose control of this situation? Did I ever have it?

I remembered when my son and daughter were young, after this type of negotiation had failed, we relied on "it's a parent's 'no.'" No more explaining. No more trying to get inside the head and heart of a child.

I can do that now, I thought, *a Susu's 'no.'*

But I didn't. Why? I'm not sure. Letting them show their physical prowess overwhelmed me perhaps. I marveled at how hard they fought for what they wanted. I sat in awe of their persuasion skills. They said what they wanted to say and then they did what they wanted to do.

I stood on solid ground looking up at their triumphant faces with eyes wide with the *yes* of daring.

To Let Others Find
Their Own Meaning

On the second shelf above my writing table, on a hexagonal stone plate, they sit, what's left of them anyway. Glass turtles, from large to small, or small to large in graduated size, like Russian dolls, one a mere shade different from the next up or down.

There used to be maybe ten, now only three left, some lost, others given away. I bought them for me, as a reminder to slow down. I bought them to remind me of the story of the tortoise and the hare. I bought them to remind me of how my slow, steady, even, Buddha-husband moves in the world, turtle-like. Nothing hurries him. He doesn't, never has, can't now, hurry himself.

When I see one of my glass turtles, I take a long deep in-breath, let out a tortoise-paced out-breath.

When I taught yoga, I'd let students choose one at the start of class. "Put one at the head of your mat," I'd say. "Yoga is not a race. We'll move slowly, deliberately, mindfully, like turtles."

I'd tiptoe from mat to mat during class, especially to those who breathed more like steam engines or semis, pulling the inhale and pushing the exhale rather than feeling respiration, trying to force rather than to allow and receive breath. I'd place my hand on a back or shoulder, put the turtle in my other hand, show it to them and take an audible slow breath. The student would match it, whole body releasing. Ahh.

On my writing table now, what's left of my collection rings a mindfulness bell, "You don't have to blast off to any finish line and miss the grass, the birds chirping, the sun sparkling or the full moon along the way or outside the window as you type or scribble."

One by one the turtles have gone. A student asked if she could have one. She'd put it on her placemat at dinner to prompt her to savor each bite. Then she'd move it to beside her sink to help her not crash through the pots and pans and to enjoy the warmth of the water, the sight of rainbows in the suds, the smell of the dish soap. "Yes," of course," I said. "Take it, have it, become it."

I gave one each to Fred and Bob. They had played with them in the bathtub each time they visited. "They are special," I'd say as I tried to explain embodied mindful yoga to them. First I demonstrated being on a mat (without being on a mat), chopping through yoga poses as if doing fast Karate. Then I'd put a tiny glass turtle on a yoga mat and dance more like a graceful ballerina. "See the difference?" I asked.

They said, "Ya, ya, can we have them?"

"You can each choose one."

Bob, the one-minute older twin, taller, more muscular, chose the teeniest turtle.

"What will you do with this turtle?" I asked Bob.

"I dunno. I'm not sure. I just love him."

I wasn't sure Bob's turtle was a him, but I was okay with love.

Fred, the shorter, one-minute younger twin, chose another tiny one. "Susu, thank you," he said.

That was months ago. I had forgotten those gifts to them, forgotten that I'd wanted those objects to mean to them what they mean to me, wanted the feel of them in their hands or even the thought of them to help them pause, breathe, stop any sibling bickering, slow the rate at which they did their third-grade multiplication homework.

One Tuesday at their home in Massachusetts, Bob came to me, hands hidden behind his back and said, "Susu, I have something to show you."

"What?" I asked.

"Guess," he said.

"Umm. M&Ms? Your soccer awards? The tooth you lost last night?"

"No, no, no. Do you want to know?"

"Of course."

He opened his hands to show the turtle, "I still have him."

Fred said, "I left mine in Maine. He likes it there."

Fred knows more than I do about how to honor that turtle. He's followed lost turtles, wanted to save them from traffic, knowing he shouldn't touch them. Fred once wanted to become a veterinarian so he could save sick turtles or endangered turtle species.

I didn't ask Bob where he keeps the turtle, what he does with him, details important to me, but not to Bob who seemed content to hold his pet, cradle him, keep him close.

I've since slowed to a turtle's pace my meaning-making for the twins.

Conclusion

Be faithful in small things because it is
in them that your strength lies.
—Mother Teresa

To Teach and To Learn

We decided to play school in their homework room. Laudie, a second-grader, perched in front of the floor-to-ceiling cloth calendar, the kind used in kindergarten rooms to teach days of the week, months of the year, the weather, how to count and the schedule for the day. Freckled Cookie and Laudie had gathered their fourteen "students" for morning meeting. Various stuffed animals sat in a crooked circle, among them one tiny bear named Fluffy. There were other bears: Pinky, Rainbow, and Elizabeth. Ellie the Elephant flopped next to me; Owl nestled near Laudie. Cookie arranged Yellows and Doggie, both dogs and Kitty. I plopped into a metal chair as Cookie shuffled the pupils to get them exactly equidistant from each other.

I learned the first rule in playing school: order.

Cookie pointed where to sit in relation to each other. "It's important," she said.

Second and third rules: everyone needs to be on the carpet, and the circle has to be round. Or maybe that's still Rule One: order.

I bent my cranky knee, crawled to the floor, and landed next to Yellows.

Laudie started, "Good morning, everyone."

She then led our class in a math exercise. She held up a square chart with numbers one to 100, fixed by rows and columns, ten times ten. "Today we are going to count by twos, fives and tens. That means we skip a certain number of numbers, the same each time. Tens are easy. Ten, twenty, thirty, forty, like that. Fives go like five, ten, fifteen, twenty. Get it?"

Fluffy fell over and toppled Ellie. Cookie straightened them out, made eye contact with them, and whispered, "No big deal. That's okay. You're fine."

Next rule: Kindness.

Laudie flipped her long blonde hair behind her back and spun it into a twist while her eyes scanned the students in her little class, not focused on anyone in particular. "Here's how you count by twos: two, four, six, eight, like that. If we are counting by twos and I say one hundred, what is the next number? Does anyone know?"

I looked around. No one volunteered. I shuffled in my seat and offered, "I think I do."

Cookie reminded me, "You have to raise your hand."

Rule: Let yourself be seen. I raised my hand. "I think I do."

Laudie, sitting tall in teacher posture, asked, "Okay, Susu, what do you think?"

I answered, "One hundred, two."

Laudie smiled, "Right. Good. Nice work."

Cookie looked at me, popped up, tromped over to me, placed her tiny hand on the wrinkled skin of my arm and sighed, "No, Susu, you are supposed to give the wrong answer. Then the teacher helps you figure it out. So, say something like seventeen or three hundred."

Learning how to be a learner, I jumbled the math in my hamster wheel brain.

"Okay, if we are counting by twos, and you want the next number after one hundred, I say it's …eighty-seven."

I also learned how to be a teacher from gentle Laudie. She patted my back. "Oh, good guess. Thank you for trying. Before you answer again let me help you. We are skipping by two each time, two, six, eight. Or twenty-two, twenty-four, twenty-six. Only two. Does that help?"

Another teaching tip: Encourage. Care.

I nodded, "Thank you. I think so. Is it….?"

Laudie interrupted, "I want to call on someone who has not spoken yet, Susu. You can wait for another turn later."

Rule: Be fair. Everyone needs a turn.

❖

I'm not sure how to end this chapter, other than to say, this chapter reminds me of the beautiful book, *All I Really Need to Know I Learned in Kindergarten* by Robert Fulghum.

I'm not sure how to end this book, either, other than to say most of what I need to know I learned, am learning and will learn from my grandchildren.

Thank you, thank you, thank you, wise teachers.

Afterword

Often when you think you're
at the end of something,
you're at the beginning of something else.
—Fred Rogers

This book bows to our great teachers, children. Further chapter titles would highlight the many more lessons they teach: Gratitude. Compassion. Open-Heartedness. Acceptance. Community. Wonder.

Imagine kids as gurus. I had wanted one mentor whose books I could read or whose retreats I could attend. Then I'd find one I liked and he or she would dole out a task I'd resist. "Wake up at 4 a.m. to mediate for an hour."

Or I'd find a good match and he or she would get teachery. "Read the classic Bhagavad-Gita for the third time from a third source."

I don't take orders well.

But teachers and teachings show up in front of us everywhere if we look.

When I started to pay attention to my life, tutors appeared: teeny grand babies whose cries for diaper changes, bottles and swaddles checkmated my ideas. Over and over. The lesson: Drop Expectations. Drop them again and again and again. Gurus demand repeated practice.

For years I have studied with these gifted instructors. I take notes. I write stories about what I've learned from the twin boys and their two sisters.

My advisors have big drive, big love, big hearts. They hug me with a big frown, "I am so sad. Why do you have to leave today?" Lesson: Unconditional Love.

They, too, insist on my rousing every day at dawn. "Susu, time to get up! We gotta finish that Lego 'struction or make sofa cushion forts." Lesson: Let Go of my Plan for Sleep. Meet the Moment.

Sometimes I forget our roles and try to force my will, "How 'bout we sit quietly and draw with these cool markers? Then maybe we could take naps."

But no. "Let's jump like bunnies to the backyard to build a stone wall and a twig bridge big enough for the turtles to go under but not so high that the rabbits trip."

The young masters speak. I pick branches and wet rocks. This is my spiritual retreat. There are no rabbits, no turtles. No matter. As I place debris around, I ask, "How big? Is this good?"

The three-year old says, "No, it's too heavy. It'll cwash. That's okay, Susu, maybe you never built a bwidge befow. Just keep pwacticing."

I want my life to go like that. With them. Following them. I want to be a student moved by the wonder in each moment's lessons. I want to laugh with the dear teachers. May the lessons continue and may adults be humble and open enough to learn them.

CPSIA information can be obtained
at www.ICGtesting.com
Printed in the USA
LVHW061258290321
682786LV00031B/487

9 781944 386528